19/11/86

Presented to the W.P. Brand

of the M.A.SA & Dr. Peter Such—

LEIPOLDT'S CAPE COOKERY

LEIPOLDT'S CAPE COOKERY

C. LOUIS LEIPOLDT

ILLUSTRATED BY
KERI SWIFT

W. J. FLESCH & PARTNERS

W. J. FLESCH & PARTNERS

P.O. BOX 3473, CAPE TOWN, 8000
P.O. BOX 3473, JOHANNESBURG, 2000

INTERNATIONAL STANDARD BOOK NUMBER
ISBN 0 949989 15 0

October 1976
Reprinted May 1983

Set in Univers 9 on 10 pt
Medium and Light
Printed and bound in South Africa by
PRINTPAK (CAPE) LTD., DACRES AVE.,
EPPING, CAPE

CONTENTS

A NOTE ON
THE AUTHOR

TODAY, like every other time, is full of fashions masquerading as the new. And one of the "in" things of the seventies is cookery. Even for men. Another is the Old Cape, even in the suburbs. Dr. Christian Louis Leipoldt was master of the Cape Table as a matter of course because he was born into the heart and soul of the South West Cape way of life, growing up as the son of a church family in the Dutch Reformed pastorie at Clanwilliam — with the Hantam district stretching away from the nearby Cedarberg, South Africa's first proclaimed Wilderness Area.

This, then, is no upstart cookery book; it is the real thing.

Leipoldt died in 1947, more than a generation ago, and the manuscript has been waiting for publication since then. However this man of immense gifts and curious contradictions was greater than his kitchen, which was only a facet of the diverse interests which he represented.

His grandfather was one of those straight-backed Rhenish Christians, full of talents and also of abnegation, who came here in 1818 and about ten years later moved to the mission station at Wupperthal. It was a small fragment of Europe lost in the mountains — and to understand Louis

7

Leipoldt, and even his cooking, one needs to go there today to tune in to remoter times.

It remains virtually untouched, like the Biedouw valley. To reach Wupperthal it is still a stoney-track pilgrimage through the outback of the Cedarberg to where the road ends with finality at that tiny land of Canaan.

Yet one must experience this nub of simple humanity and green things — lost at the bottom of a harsh whirlpool of rock slabs, high sky and palpitating summer heat — to properly appreciate against today's unreality Leipoldt's charming chronicle of the Cape's culinary civilisation.

To emerge and grow in the biblical severity of a German mission background was to become either a troglodyte or an intellectual. Like Jan Smuts, in another part of the Platteland, Leipoldt was forged and honed by this environment and experience to the sharpest perception. And the European strain came through strongly in his acute mind, which ran free and untrammelled. All sorts would want to claim him as their own but, puckishly, he escaped every grasping hand.

Nevertheless, he was a deep and true expositor of the post-Boer War Afrikaner gees, and the abiding skuilplek of his innermost soul was always the Clanwilliam mountain spine — this ragged place, the wide place, the so-far-from-cities place, the place so heavenly in spring . . .

'n Handvol gruis uit the Hantam —
My liewe, lekker Hantam-wyk!
'n Handvol gruis en gedroogte blare,
Waboom-blare, ghnarrabos-blare!
Arm was ek gister, en nou is ek ryk.

Above all things he will be remembered as a poet. . . .

No wonder they buried him in a shallow cave, near a freshet of mountain water, among the torn and rufous crags of the Pakhuis Pass. Faded Bushman paintings can still be seen on the rock-face; and these other little poets, who also wandered lonely as a cloud along the uplands, probably watch attentively over his spirit when, late at night, the limousines and the bakkies stop rushing past on the wide new hoofpad.

With our new awakening to Cape furniture, Cape cooking, to the simple refinements of our farm-orientated architecture of the past, it is good that this book gives an opportunity to remember him in an English context, because his awareness was all-embracing, not tribal. He who felt so fulfilled at Clanwilliam and its world of mountains also moved easily through the wider world.

His distinctions in medicine and surgery came from Britain, Germany, America and Austria. He once even spent six months at sea in a luxury steam-yacht, having fun as a sort of intellectual punch-bag for the eccentric American publisher Joseph Pulitzer. Ostensibly he was to be the millionaire's medical man, but Pulitzer required his doctor to be "tall, with a good reading voice, literary tastes, a knowledge of languages, placid, never seasick and, if possible, musical." Professional ability, it seemed, was at a discount but the salary offered was princely.

At Guys Hospital, London, in 1907 the young Leipoldt

8

won the Treasurer's Gold Medal in both surgery and medicine and only two years later he was a Fellow of the Royal College of Surgeons. He was still an undergraduate when he became the editor of Sir Henry Burdett's medical weekly. Much later in South Africa, among many other activities, he guided the *South African Medical Journal* and was secretary to the South African Medical Association.

He once stood for Parliament in the Wonderboom constituency in the Transvaal; in another direction, he was mentioned in dispatches on the staff of General Botha in World War 1. But the literary bent was already there in early childhood. Ink was his first wine. He tried his hand at tragedy, on the theme of Akbar, at the age of eight in Clanwilliam; and at 13 a story of his appeared in the *Cape Argus*, after he had also won a competition in the *Boy's Own Paper* 6 000 miles away.

In his sixties he took to the radio like a duck to water and was a regular of the SABC's then-famous Question Time programme.

His Afrikaans cook-book *Kos vir die Kenner* is a classic in that language, yet he prepared this present, entirely-separate manuscript in English just before he died. In this last period he had published much poetry in English under the pseudonym of Pheidippides. He was busy, too, on a book on President Kruger, which he had first projected in the first decade of the century, to explain and justify the old man of the Transvaal Republic to an international English-language audience.

This work was far advanced when his heart finally faltered in April 1947. He asked to be taken to die in the Clanwilliam district, but this was impossible, and only his ashes found their way back to his early stamping ground.

The Cape Table is published now at the instigation of his literary executor, Dr. Peter Shields, who was one of the young boys brought up and educated in Cape Town as wards of Louis Leipoldt. As a member of his household at Arbury, Kenilworth, for many years, Dr. Shields has vivid memories of Leipoldt the human catalyst, the whimsical dispenser of controversy and paradox as a tonic for the stodgy-minded.

Leipoldt was one of our earliest true appreciators of wine as an adornment of the table and his anti-teetotal campaign, to encourage the judicious use of good wines in infant diet instead of milk, is still recalled and relished by many. Little known, however, is the fact that some of his best-loved poetry in Afrikaans was first set down in English — but in those days the main market in South Africa where hard cash was paid and publication was assured for verse was in Afrikaans.

Naturally, he converted these literary assets into the hardest currency. His chief tool of communication was English, but his greatest literary felicities were undoubtedly in Afrikaans where his ear and his sight for the fine-flavoured written word was sharpest.

Knowing the piquant background to this wonderfully versatile man, his flavour as well as that of the authentic

Cape Table pervades this volume.

As an anti-pedant, he eschews finicking precision about quantities. Let others write medical prescriptions for food, instead of cultivating their flair. He goes to all sorts of (perhaps unconscious) lengths to avoid the gram and the ounce. Instead we find phrases like a hint of this or that — a sprig, a scattering, a pinch, "collect as many limpets off the rocks as your backache allows," a morsel of tangerine peel, a blade of mace, a slither of cinnamon, a feathering of some other goodie, a scrap of this, some flicks of that. . . .

To a gushing woman who asked him how to prepare a quail he replied with great unction: "Dress a large turkey and place inside of it a korhaan; inside of this a chicken which can enfold a partridge. Within the partridge place your quail. Season well and bake and baste with care. Your quail will emerge with unbelieveable succulence when you have discarded the rest. . . ." He stomped off as she stewed in confusion.

To editors who came seeking an explanation of significant passages in his work he would cry out testily: "How should I know what I meant; that is your job." When another respectfully pointed out that a sonnet was missing two lines, obviously left out when the typist did the transcription, he shrugged. "Ag man, you know what I was driving at. Knock off the lines yourself or drop the lot in the wastepaper basket. . . ."

To these people hovering on the creative fringes he was a disturbing, colourful, if scholarly extrovert. Essentially, however, he was a touch-me-not loner. His private world was a place apart where the values were too plangent for common traffic. Again like Jan Christiaan Smuts, it was somewhere there up among the mountains.

As one who has also dossed down under the stars in the Cedarberg and the Biedouw in the company of another Afrikaner with a thorn-skerm round his soul, the artist Francois Krige — and been wrung by deep atavistic chords up there along the high paths — I hope some will accept this book as a little more than just another essay on today's rather chic cookery thing. Its writer represents a rare vintage year in the crop of South Africans.

BRIAN LELLO
Oude Raapkraal

INTRODUCTION

MY interest in cookery dates from the time when, as a little boy in the late eighties of the last century, I assisted, in a very minor and suppressed capacity, at the culinary operations of a very expert Coloured woman çook who bore the reputation of being one of the best in the Cape Colony. Fat to the verge of obesity, she presided over a kitchen whose cleanliness could have served as a model for an operating theatre of a modern hospital, largely because she insisted that punctilious, painstaking ablution was an indispensable preliminary in the preparation of food. Her inculcation of these elementary principles, often accompanied by a good-natured but nevertheless painful prodding of my juvenile person with the large wooden spoon that was her sceptre, helped me — in later days when I learned to better my taste and broaden my experience — to realise how any infringement of them inevitably impairs the excellence of all cookery.

The Ayah's art was the result of many years of instruction and experience in the traditional methods of Malay cookery, whose outstanding characteristics are the free, almost heroic, use of spices and aromatic flavourings, the prolonged steady, but slow, application of moist heat to all meat dishes, and the skilful blending of many diverse constituents into a combination that still holds the essential goodness of each. Her dishes, that were eaten by Governors, Prime Ministers and Very Important Persons, were made from old recipes that were firmly enshrined in her memory, for she never referred to written or printed directives. Nearly every one of these recipes is to be found in cookery books that were then already well known — without, however, the little modifications that her own ingenuity and experience had enabled her to add for their improvement. All of them had already been written down, in manuscripts for domestic use for those who had to rely on such aids when preparing food.

When I returned from Europe in 1914, it was a labour of love to collect such cookery manuscripts, and to compare what they contained with the printed collections of directives that date from the year 1483. That entailed the acquisition of representative cook books, and although I had, at the time, no intention of emulating Viel or any other great collector of books on food and drink, I found the task of comparing and collating so entrancing, the

11

search for recipes in manuscript so exciting, and the pride of possessing interesting rarities so uplifting, that what had begun as a passing fancy remained as a serious and not altogether unproductive study.

Some of the results I have tried to epitomise in this book. It does not claim to be exhaustive. There are thousands of recipes for preparing food; but those that may presume to merit the prefix of a regional adjective, by reason of their insistence on some local method of blending or cooking, are far fewer than is commonly supposed. The art of the cook is international in its general application, and only in particulars, and more especially in the use of local ingredients, does the cookery of one nation or country differ from that of its neighbours. The recipes that I have included here are those that have been in vogue in South Africa from the earliest times, and are nearly all variations of similar ones that were popular in Europe and the East. But most of them have been modified, and many of them have been immensely improved, by the skill and experience of Cape cooks, while there are some that have been adapted to local foodstuffs that are found nowhere else. In the majority of cases the original text has been followed as closely as possible, and where it has been necessary to translate from the Dutch the interpretation has been textual.

No attempt has been made to transcribe the great number of recipes for cakes and confectionery, of which there are many in manuscript and quite enough in print. With few exceptions they are merely replicas of familiar European directives, possibly with some slight modifications to which a new name has been given. A good example of such plagiarism is the number of fruit or spice cakes that figure under the names of some local celebrity, but that are not justified in claiming any merit for originality. Where a particular kind of cake or confectionery is required to be served as an accompaniment to a sweet or a meat dish, directions for its preparation are given.

Similarly nothing has been said about aboriginal cookery. Undoubtedly the Africans have modified some methods of preparing food, but so far as I know, no one has as yet attempted to collect their recipes or describe their methods. There is undoubtedly sufficient material to warrant such a compilation, but its collecting and editing must be left to the industrious inquiry of a student fully conversant with African languages and customs.

Nor has it seemed necessary to attach a bibliography, or to indicate, by footnotes, the source of some of the references. It may, however, be mentioned that all the "literature" from which this book has been compiled is to be found in the collection of cookery books in the South African Public Library at Cape Town, which also contains most of the manuscripts from which the recipes have been extracted. Most of the latter have already been published, in Afrikaans, in my own cookery book, *Kos vir die Kenner*, that was issued in 1933.

C. LOUIS LEIPOLDT
Cape Town, December 1946.

12

Chapter 1

ORIGINS OF CAPE COOKERY

THE settlement at the Cape of Good Hope was started in 1652 as a revictualing station for the ships of the East India Company of Holland trading between the mother country and the East. In the course of time it became the half-way house on the great 6 000-mile sea route from the Texel, the Thames and the Tagus in the north, to Colombo and Calcutta, Tandjong Priok and Tonkin in the south. Its few hundred inhabitants increased to several thousands, augmented by immigrants from Europe, Chinese convicts and state prisoners from Java and slaves from Mozambique, with the result that the straggling town, under the shadow of its imposing mountain, acquired an almost cosmopolitan character that was to have its influence on the habits and customs of its citizens.

Nowhere was this influence to be more recognisable, even although its effects were insidious and not immediately apparent, than in the methods and ways of preparing food for the table. What we may today call "Cape cookery" is characterised, not by a wholly original,

origins intrinsically national quality, but by a subtle combination of various and diverse fashions in cooking, adapted and modified from many different countries, to which the use of certain locally-grown ingredients has given a new and peculiar tinge. As the patient Mentzel has told us, the Chinese cooks at the Cape were celebrated, even in their rude and vulgar little chop shops, for their extreme cleanliness and the fastidiousness with which they prepared their succulent dishes. Mrs Kindersley, some years later, commented on the variety of spices that were considered necessary in a Cape kitchen, while many other visitors testified at times to the strangeness but more often to the savouriness of the viands that they tasted at private houses or at public eating-places.

While there is no dish, with the exception of those for the preparation of which the main ingredient must be something that can be procured only in South Africa, that can be considered peculiar to the Cape, in so far as its replica cannot be found elsewhere, there are many Cape cookery recipes that have been evolved from prototypes in old European cookery books. But they have been so changed, and possibly improved, by local methods that the dishes prepared from them can be said to possess a distinctive and peculiarly local excellence.

The foundations of Cape cookery, like those of the cookery of all western nations, are the methods that have descended to us from the Greek and Roman civilisation, which through the centuries have been altered, elaborated and bettered by cooks in various European countries, whose orginality and ingenuity, imagination and expert skill have evolved systems that are of national significance. It is impossible today to adjudicate on the claims for priority made by these varied systems. After all, the oldest cookery book with a right to be considered as an exposition of the art of cooking is the early Chinese compilation, far antedating any Greek papyrus, that gives admirable recipes for cooking rice and making stews. However, Atheaeus tells us that Agis, the Rhodian cook, first discovered how to roast fish; Charides, the Athenian, to make forcemeat; Aphthonetus to broil sausages; and Lamprias to concoct a palatable soup. But there is no evidence that any of his seven pre-eminent chefs created a special system of Greek cookery.

The truth of the matter is that the cookery of every nation has borrowed freely, often with unblushing audacity, from that of every other nation, and that only where it has succeeded in impressing its own stamp on its cooking technique, by the practice of local methods and the employment of local foodstuffs, can it be said to have reached the level that merits a distinctive territorial adjective.

Bearing this truth in mind, we can readily understand how much Cape cookery owes to Dutch, Flemish, English, German, French, Italian, Portuguese and especially Oriental cookery. Its indebtedness to Russian, Swedish, Danish or American cookery is negligible, has been incurred only in recent years and cannot be said to have benefited it. What is good in American cookery, for

14

instance, derives from practically the same sources as Cape **origins** cookery and there is in some respects a cousinship between the two, for both owe much to Dutch and Flemish influence.

As the early settlers at the Cape came from Holland it is not surprising that Dutch influence in Cape cookery should be considerable, although it does not overshadow that of Oriental cookery. At the time when Van Riebeeck landed — that is, in the middle of the seventeenth century — there was no defined system of Dutch cookery, but domestic cookery in the lowlands had already developed methods and dishes that were different from those in neighbouring countries. The art of cookery in Holland, as indeed in every country in Europe, was largely influenced by Italian cooks, for in the Middle Ages Italian cooks were considered the masters of the craft and the Vatican cooks were ranked as the best in the world. Later French cuisine increased in estimation, and to a large extent supplanted Italian cookery. In Flanders and in Holland, at the time when European civilisation was best exemplified by the cultural and economic expansion of these countries, cookery, as an art, had rapidly developed and had assimilated and adapted the best that was to be found in the cookery of neighbouring nations.

The first cookery books in South Africa, as also in Europe, were manuscript collections of domestic recipes, of traditional methods of preparing food, and of household directions, home remedies and rules of health. One of the best-known European manuscripts is that of William Tirel, called Taillevent, copies of which are now in the Vatican Library and in the National Library at Paris. Taillevent was cook to King Charles V from 1373 to 1387, and his recipes were edited and republished by Baron Pichon and Georges Vicaire in 1891. Another contemporary collection of culinary recipes is that of the Master Cook of Richard II of England, compiled in 1390, known to cooks under the title of *The Forme of Cury*. Many other such collections of recipes are known to exist in various forms.

In South Africa there are several manuscript cookery books, the earliest, in the South African Public Library at Cape Town, dating to the fifteenth century, with copious additions, in various handwritings, extending into the sixteenth and seventeenth centuries. These manuscripts were undoubtedly brought into the country as family treasures, carefully preserved and judiciously expanded by their owners. Similar manuscript collections were started in the eighteenth and early part of the nineteenth century by local housewives, containing original recipes and copies of those already published. In the latter part of the seventeenth century the number of printed cookery books in Europe greatly increased, while their prices were low enough to win them a wide and deserved popularity. Every housewife could buy one, and thus it was scarcely necessary to compile a private collection of recipes for each household.

At the Cape, however, such printed works were always relatively scarce, and it is interesting to note that among

15

origins the books in the largest private collection at the time when the Cape was still in possession of the Dutch there is not a single copy of a printed cookery book.

The South African Public Library does possess a varied collection of cookery books, but few of its finest volumes were procured from local sources. The oldest book in the collection was printed in 1517 at the Strassburg press of Johannes Knoblouch. It is a later edition of the first cookery book ever printed, the *De Honesta Voluptate et Valetudine* of Baptista Platina, of which the first edition appeared in 1479. It was exceedingly popular and went through many editions and, in 1528, a French translation was published at Lyons. Compiled by a practical cook, who was an artist and no mean scholar, it was a useful, readable and interesting epitome of the art of cookery in the fourteenth century and contained more than 300 recipes. As the earliest printed cookery book it merits the attention of every student of the art, for in it is enshrined the original conception of everything that is good in modern cookery.

South African cooks are unlikely ever to have read it. Nor is it reasonable to believe that they had any acquaintance with the works of Platina's many successors that came tumbling from European printing presses in the next 200 years. But in the eighteenth century Dutch, German and French books on cookery were to be found at the Cape. Among these, Christian Sachsstadter's treatise on the cookery of fish undoubtedly gave many suggestions to our cooks, as the manuscript collections of recipes prove, while the works of Dankwerth, Eger, Cocceius and especially the standard *Le Cuisinier Moderne* of the famous Vincent la Chapelle, cook in the Prince of Orange's household, were frequently and usefully consulted. This last book, with the anonymous but extremely practical *Verstandighe Kock* which, published at the end of the seventeenth century, gave a clear account of Flemish and Dutch cookery, served for many years as a reservoir from which all subsequent compilers freely watered their culinary nurseries.

Much later writers in Holland and England drew on the knowledge of visitors to the East, who brought back with them directions for making dishes that were not included in the older inventories. English cookery books of the early eighteenth century gave directions for preparing Indian dishes, but only in the first half of the nineteenth century do we come across recipes that are of purely local origin, although even here there is some doubt about the matter. We must bear in mind the fact that the contact between West and East dates back to far beyond the time of Platina and Scappi. The Crusades had already introduced oriental spices and eastern ways of preparing food for the table into occidental kitchens.

Hashed meat, baked with a curried sauce, spiced with red pepper and sweetened with blanched almonds, exactly similar to the modern *bobotie* of Cape cookery, was well known to the old Italian cooks. Savoury dried meat, the South African *biltong*, or, in its more primitive

16

form, the Dutch *tassal*, was prepared by the peasants in
the Adour valley when that part of France was still regarded
as an English possession — and is still so made in Switzer-
land. The vegetable and meat stews, known as *bredies* to
Cape cooks, were old favourites of the Greek chefs,
whose name for them is so totally unpronounceable that I
have never yet come across a modern Greek who can say it
without stuttering.

The two recipes quoted in a late edition of Mrs Rundle's
Domestic Economy and Cookery, first published in 1827
and later edited and amplified by Miss Morris, who had
visited the Cape, are, however, so distinctly South African
and entail the use of ingredients hardly likely to be popular,
or even procurable, in England, that one can safely assume
that they were directly transcribed from manuscript recipes
consulted at Cape Town. This assumption is strengthened
by the names given to the dishes, which include a word
not to be found in an ordinary English dictionary though
perfectly well known to every English-speaking housewife
then living at the Cape.

It may be added, in passing, that no printed book on
Cape cookery has included these recipes, although they
are to be found, with variations not mentioned by Miss
Morris, in several manuscript collections and are almost
traditional at the Cape.

Undoubtedly the most potent influence on Cape
cookery has been the methods, tastes and culinary customs of the Malay cooks brought directly from Java in
the early part of the eighteenth century. Mr Spenser St.
John, in his entertaining book, *Life in the Forests of the
Far East*, published in the latter part of the past century,
has paid a well-deserved compliment to his Malay cook:

Malay cookery is sometimes very tasty; I remember
spending a fortnight in the Sultan's palace, and we were
fed daily from his kitchen; sometimes the stewed fowls
were admirable and there was a particular kind of rice-
cake, sent in very hot, which was delicious. But the
triumph of Malay cookery is to send in the sambals in
perfection, particularly the one called blachang; the best
is composed of the very finest prawns, caught, I imagine,
soon after the little ones have burst from their eggs, and
pounded up with red chillies and a little ginger. Coarser
kinds are made from the larger prawn, or even from the
smallest fish caught on the river's banks. Sometimes the
material is first exposed to the sun in order to be completely
dried, or it would not keep or mix very well, though it is
often soaked till nearly decomposed, and that is perhaps
the favourite way when it emits a rather powerful scent,
but it is very tasty. Prawns and fish are cooked in a great
variety of ways, but roasting them over a fire as kebabs, is
an excellent fashion if you first sprinkle them with curry
mixture . . .

I have mentioned the admirable curry which Ahtan put
before me; perhaps I ought to explain how we make that
dish in the Far East; it appears a very different thing from
what I have tasted in England under the name of curry. A

fowl is cut up into small pieces, and four dried and two green onions, five chillies, half a turmeric, one teaspoonful of coriander seed, one of white cumin, and one of sweet cumin, are provided. You must well pound the seeds, turmeric and chillies, and slice the onions fine; then take the saucepan, and after buttering it, slightly brown the onions, then add the pounded ingredients with just sufficient water to reduce them to a paste, and throw in the fowl and well mix them up, till the meat has a yellow tint, and lastly, add the cocoa-nut milk, and boil till the curry be thoroughly cooked ... The cocoa-nut milk is made by scraping the meat of half an old nut very fine, then soaking it in warm water, and after squeezing out the milk, throw the fibre away.

These directions are identical with those of some of our earliest manuscript recipes, and show how closely East Indian methods were followed at the Cape, even though the *blachang* referred to is obviously a mistake for the much more pungent *trassi* condiment that never became naturalised anywhere outside the Malay archipelago. At first nearly all the necessary ingredients for preparing Indian dishes had to be imported; later on the settlement grew its own rice, chillies, ginger, cumin, coriander and garlic, but it still had to get its tamarind, turmeric, black pepper, mace, nutmeg, saffron, cinnamon and coconuts from the East. It was customary for Cape housewives to commission captains of ships going to Batavia to buy and bring back modest quantities of these spices and delicacies. A domestic account book of the early part of the past century gives a list of the prices paid for such things, and includes among them "candy sugar; black moist sugar; birds-nests; dried prawns; dessicated sea urchins".

The Malay community at the Cape has always had a reputation for its good cookery and even now the best women cooks are to be found among the Coloured people who have been trained to appreciate all that is best in both eastern and western culinary fashions. In the old days a Malay cook was regarded as indispensable for the house-household that wished to entertain; slaves who had knowledge of this kind of cookery commanded a far higher price than other domestic chattels. Thus a local advertisement stated that "Malani, a good cook, exceptionally skilled and not wasteful in the kitchen", was one of five slaves to be sold on behalf of the estate of a deceased owner; while an account of a slave auction related that "there was spirited competition for Emerentia, who is an acknowledged artist of the pot". At the hospitable house where the young officer, later on to be Lord Wellington the conqueror of Napoleon but at that time rusticating on his way to India, was frequently entertained by the richest man in Cape Town, the cook was a coloured woman, skilled in the preparation of oriental dishes and ably supported by her husband who acted as butler.

Oriental influence, indeed, was predominant in Cape cookery, and its importance can easily be judged by the value attached to eastern spices and condiments in the **origins** old fashioned recipes.

The first printed collection of such recipes published at the Cape is today perhaps one of the rarest items of Africana known to exist, for only one copy, that in the South African Public Library, has survived the tribulations that seem to make the life of the average cookery book much shorter that that of its owner. It is a small octavo pamphlet, printed by a Pietermaritzburg firm in Natal, in the early seventies of the past century. It gives, in English, a series

of recipes none of which can be said to be peculiarly South African, as their originals are all to be found in works published in Europe before that date. It is possible that an earlier collection of recipes was published, also in pamphlet form, at Cape Town, some years before the Natal publication, but no specimen of this has survived.* From the beginning of the nineteenth century, newspapers and periodicals in English and Dutch, and later in Afrikaans, had printed family and domestic recipes, but no one had thought it worth while to collect them for reprinting in book form, probably because there was no demand for a volume on local cookery as every housewife possessed her own collection of manuscript recipes, or relied on her training and memory for her cooking. The publication of the obscure and incomplete compilation in Natal must have aroused some interest, for although it was never reprinted it was soon followed by a much more authoritative little book which even today may be consulted with advantage as it is a thoroughly trustworthy, clear and concise epitome of Cape cookery.

This was Miss A. G. Hewitt's *Cape Cookery*, a small octavo, 88-page volume, published by Darter Bros. and Walton of Cape Town in 1889, of which a second and final edition was published in the following year. Although it included several recipes that were extracted from overseas cookery books, it gave the first accurate account of many local recipes, assembled under five headings. The first chapter was devoted to fish, and gave directions for

*There is mention of such a collection in the headnote to a recipe "Taken from Messrs. Cleghorns book".

origins the preparation of such dishes as *smoored kreef; stewed klipkous; ingelegde fish; snoek pekelaar; smoored snoek;* and *kreef salad.* These are generally correct, although it may be pointed out that bones are used to enrich the pearl mussel* stew, which is quite unnecessary, and that water is added, which makes the meat tough; while the braised snoek is made without potatoes and the crayfish salad omits the savoury portions to be found under the carapace as well as the coral. The second chapter deals with meat and poultry, and gives recipes for preparing *roast meat or poultry in the baking pot; hoender pastei; zout ribbetjie; bobotee; sassaties; ingelegde kop en pootjies; tomato, quince, bean, pumpkin, cauliflower and cabbage bredies; porcupine skin; Cape curry* and *biltong.*

By following Miss Hewitt's directions most of these dishes can be made without difficulty, but some of them will lack the savoury excellence to which they are entitled.

In the third chapter sweet dishes are discussed; in the fourth, preserves, and in the fifth a number of miscellaneous recipes are given, among them being *sambal; blatjang, Cape chutney, sea-weed blancmange; apricot vinegar, peach pickle, penguin eggs,* and *Van der Hum liqueur.* The little book is a model of conciseness, but entirely lacking in character and distinction, while it errs on the side of frugality and plainness, eschewing the use of wine and spices in places where these are regarded as indispensable in the older manuscript recipes. It is, however, a useful compilation and was deservedly popular in its day, although it could not claim that it was an exhaustive collection of Cape recipes, nor that it gave the reader copies of the best to be found in the old family manuscript cook books.

Contemporaneously with it appeared Mrs A. R. Barnes' *Colonial Household Guide,* by A. R. B., published by the same firm as an octavo volume of 150 pages. It contained, besides many cookery recipes, most of which are taken from printed works, farming and household hints, home remedies and directions for preparing cleaning and polishing materials. The only recipes that can be said to be of local origin were those that dealt with *Keokuk toast; cabbage bredie; soesaties; baba* or *barble fish; wild buck; green mealies* and *sweet potatoes.* Even these are poor, and if scrupulously followed will hardly prepare dishes that are worthy of their titles. As a guide to Cape cookery, Mrs Barnes' book is much inferior to Miss Hewitt's.

Both were soon afterwards followed, and altogether displaced, by an authoritative and comprehensive work on Cape cookery that for a long time remained the standard book on the subject and may even now be consulted with advantage as a thoroughly trustworthy and excellently written and annotated collection of Cape cookery recipes.

This was *Hilda's Where is It?,* published by Chapman and Hall of London in 1891, which before 1908 had sold

---

*Venus ear or perlemoen.

24 000 copies and had reached its nineteenth edition. Its **origins** authoress was Miss Hildagonda Johanna Duckitt, who assured her readers that the book contained "amongst other practical and tried recipes, many old Cape, Indian, and Malay Dishes and Preserves; also Directions for polishing Furniture, cleaning Silk etc. and a Collection of Home Remedies in case of Sickness", all in rigid accordance with the then prevailing fashion in cookery books. The volume was interleaved with blank pages for manuscript recipes and had attached to it a neat little lead pencil for the convenience of transcribers.

Miss Duckitt, in her *Diary of a Cape Housekeeper* – published in 1902, and in some ways a more interesting and original work than her first book – gave details about her background that proved her to be fully justified in undertaking to speak on behalf of Cape cooks. Her grandfather, William Duckitt, of the Treasurer-General's departmet in London, accepted an offer from the Cape administration to come out and supervise the establishment of model farms under the newly-formed Department of Agriculture in the early part of the past century. He brought with him his family, a staff of 30 servants and pedigree sheep and cattle, together with various agricultural gadgets that he had invented for the better cultivation of hard soils. The wine farmers in the western districts of the Cape are indebted to him for much good advice and many practical demonstrations, but in 1839 he tired of government service, and settled on his own farm, Groot Pos, in the Malmesbury district, an estate that had been developed and improved by Lord Charles Somerset. His sons married into colonial families. Miss Duckitt's father espoused Hildagonda Versfeld, and so became allied to several of the oldest and best Dutch families at the Cape – for the most part wealthy wine and wheat farmers, who lived in comfortable affluence, served by many slaves and priding themselves on their unstinted hospitality and the quality of their fare. On the farm where Miss Duckitt spent her childhood, the cook was an East Indian, an adept at making curry and Malay dishes, who had also learned to prepare food in accordance with traditional Dutch methods. From her relations and friends she learned many household secrets, had access to the family collections of recipes that were then the substitutes for printed cookery books and received, as was customary in those days, a sound education in housekeeping and domestic economy. She was thus admirably fitted to write what for a long time was to remain the soundest and most authoritative manual on Cape cookery.

Her *Hilda's Where is It?* contains about 150 recipes that are characteristically South African, inasmuch as they are modifications, improvements or adaptations of European recipes. About 50 others are exclusively South African in so far as the preparation of the ingredients is totally different from that recommended in then existing cookery books. These latter show the influence of Oriental cooking methods, combined with local ingenuity in blending flavours and enhancing the savour of the dish.

21

Unfortunately the book contains no recipes for the peculiarly South African dishes manufactured from ingredients that are essentially local — such as water hawthorn stew and the purees made from veld plants — and omits some of the recipes to be found in manuscript collections. She made no pretence to catholicity, and her directions are everywhere so clear and precise — as for example where she deals with the preparation of *Haliotis* mussel* and emphasises the necessity to avoid adding water to the dish — that her book may be accepted as an authoritative practical guide to Cape cookery.

The first Afrikaans cookery book was published about the same time as Miss Duckitt's manual, by the *Patriot* publishers at the Paarl. It was a compilation by Mrs E. J. Dijkman of the Orange Free State, and was translated, badly, into English in 1905. It went into several editions, and enjoyed a large measure of popularity, not so much on account of its cookery recipes but because it contained many hints on first aid and household remedies, some of the latter being strange but harmless. In comparison with Miss Duckitt's book it is greatly inferior; most of its recipes are merely transcriptions from familiar Dutch cookery books, and the few really South African ones are of minor importance. One misses in it any reference to the popular "veld food" dishes, while the chapter on fish is singularly incomplete. The book is a mere compilation by one who had had some experience of plain domestic cookery, but who had not been accustomed to any great variety and is not an expert in the true sense of the term. Mrs. Dijkman gives fancy names to some of her concoctions. There are for instance, "Afrikander Bond", "President Kruger", "President Steyn", "General de la Rey" and "General Botha" cakes, which are nothing more than variations of ordinary fruit cakes. If some of her directions are to be followed precisely, as for example in the recipe for stewing pearl mussel, the resulting dish is likely to be far from satisfactory. Her cookery is economical, even parsimonious, and she is frugal in her employment of wine and spices, with the result that her dishes, if not insipid, sometimes lack the fragrant pungency that they ought to have.

From the beginning of the twentieth century the number of books on Cape cookery steadily increased. There are today many well known manuals. Most of these are merely compilations, while in some modern American methods are adapted to South African ingredients, not always with the best results.

Perhaps the most striking feature about these newer books on Cape cookery is the total omission of wine in the recipes, and the neglect to produce something that is original, either in blending or in using local ingredients that will give a distinct flavour to the dishes. Domestic cookery is taught in girls' schools, but it is indoctrinated in accordance with a syllabus that does not in the slightest degree arouse the interest of the cook or the lover of good

*Venus Ear or pearl mussel.

food. Moreover old methods of cooking are neglected in **origins** favour of the pestilential but handy and convenient electric stove; the open fireplace is almost a thing of the past. Another cause of the decay of Cape cookery is the popularity of tinned and dehydrated food and of the ready-made bottled sauce and salad dressing. But undoubtedly the most important reason for the lack of development and the absence of originality is the ignorance of professional as well as domestic cooks of the old and tried methods and recipes that in the past century made Cape cookery an art that was justified in claiming a technique and a merit of its own.

Chapter II

METHODS OF COOKING

PROPERLY speaking, the art of cookery is the art of preparing food for eating by cooking it, that is to say, by rendering it more palatable through the application of heat. In practice, however, the art of cookery includes much more than that, for it embraces all methods of preparing food for the table, even those in which no attempt is made to vary the character of the crude ingredients except by the addition of flavouring or the subtraction of what interferes with the palatability.

Nevertheless heat, in its various forms, is the chief means whereby raw natural food can be suitably modified to serve human needs by making it more eatable, digestible and nourishing. It may be applied in various forms, directly or indirectly, and a predilection for one or more of these different ways of using it may perhaps be a distinguishing feature between two systems of national cookery. Among peoples who lack the amenities provided by a more sophisticated domestic culture, such as stoves and ovens, the open fire, on a flat hearth or in some sheltered spot of the garth, is the main (and sometimes the only) means of cooking. The result is that roasting broiling and grilling have been more highly developed in **methods** these communities than other methods of cooking.

In Cape cookery, which developed when the settlement was still primitive and was largely influenced by Oriental methods and to some extent by the rough technique employed in the ship's caboose, all forms of heat are used – though there is a preference for direct application of heat, especially to meats and to edibles that have a resistant covering. The three principal ways of applying such heat are roasting, baking and grilling or broiling, in all of which the food is subjected to the direct action of fire or to such action communicated through the intermediary of a pot or pan or oven.

In *boiling;* which is another essential way of cooking, the heat is communicated to the foodstuff through the intermediary of water that has been raised to a high, or boiling, temperature ; in frying, oil is substituted for water, but the principle remains the same. In both boiling and frying a part of the flavour and nutritive quality of the food may be lost, because it is taken up by the water or the oil. It is therefore necessary to stop for a moment to consider what actually occurs when either of these methods is used, to compare their advantages with other methods in which direct heat is employed.

When a foodstuff is placed in water and that water is brought to the boil, some part of the soluble ingredients in the food is dissolved in the water. The result is that when the food has been cooked it has lost that portion of its contents which is now to be found in the water in which it has been boiled. In frying, this is less often of importance, because oil is not a good solvent and the heat of the oil usually coats the foodstuff with an impermeable film through which its soluble content cannot percolate. We take advantage of this when we make soup or extracts. The foodstuff is placed in water which is brought to the boil, and then slowly simmered, so as to extract from the food as much of its soluble content as is possible.

In that way we obtain a soup, which is in reality a decoction of foodstuffs.

If, however, we wish to have the foodstuff boiled for itself, it is necessary to plunge it into boiling water, the heat of which at once solidifies the surface into a protective film behind which the soluble contents may be allowed to cook steadily until the food itself is tender. The old cooks understood this perfectly and in Cape recipes a clear distinction is always drawn between boiling to extract the soluble content of the food – in which it is always recommended that cold or lukewarm water should be used and generally heated – and boiling to make the food itself more palatable.

By *roasting,* the Cape cook did not mean spit roasting, although this method was sometimes employed, especially in the kitchens of the large town houses where the hearths were big enough to permit the installation of a turning jack or spit. Properly speaking roasting is by exposure of the foodstuff to the direct action of fire, which is tempered, to prevent scorching, by the basting juice with which the

25

methods food is constantly wetted. This method gives admirable results, and has been a favourite with English cooks, whose roasts have been extolled by all who have tasted them. But it is a laborious and expensive method, which demands constant attention on the part of the cook, and the excellence of the results obtained by it depends to a large extent on the quality of the meat. At the Cape beef has never been of prime excellence, and the domestic cook had much more to attend to than to waste time turning the jack and painstakingly dripping basting juice over the joint.

With meat that was indifferent in quality, an equally good result was obtainable by *pot-roasting*, in which the food was placed in an iron pot with a heavy iron lid. All this was put on the fire and live coals or embers were heaped on the lid. Occasionally the lid was lifted and the food was basted, but as its exuding juice remained in the pot, there was no necessity for a roasting pan and no reason to fear that it would scorch. It was subjected to a steady, equable heat, that cooked it nicely and made even the toughest goat-mutton tender. Pot roasting was a popular method of cooking, and was indeed the only method generally used, although oven roasts, in which the meat was baked, were later on more fashionable and seem to be preferred today.

The pot roast was economical, timesaving, and satisfactory. In course of time its principle was extended to other methods, of which *smooring* (literally, smothering) or *smoorbraai* (stew-roasting) was the chief modification. This is the old-fashioned braising, in which the food was stewed or braised by heat applied from above and below, and was used chiefly for combinations of meat and vegetables. *Bredies*, for instance, are always carefully and slowly smothered — and the longer this gentle and persuasive manner of cooking is applied the better and more savoury will be the result of the stew, provided care is taken, by frequently shaking the pot, to prevent the contents from burning.

Stewing and *steaming* were further modifications of applying indirect heat, and both were much employed by Cape cooks ; fish, for instance, was generally steamed, usually with a spoonful of white wine to hasten the cooking and give piquancy to the dish.

For meats, fish, and some vegetables, a favourite method of preparation was *grilling* directly over the hot embers, either on a spit or on a grid. Nothing can exceed in savouriness a tender mutton chop grilled over the embers of a rhinoceros-bush fire. The aromatic flavour of the smoke imparts to the meat a peculiar and altogether original taste, and if a good camp cook is in charge of the business the "carbonade" is as delicious as it is tender and succulent.

All *kabobs* should be grilled, but nowadays when one has to depend on a coal fire, it is not easy to resist the temptation to cook them in the oven in a pan, or fry them on the stove. Old Cape cooks never used coal, a fuel that was exclusively reserved for blacksmiths and never became

26

popular in domestic kitchens before the arrival of steam- **methods**
ships. They used firewood, of which the supply never
failed or, when they could get it, charcoal that still provides
the finest heat for grilling.

Almost as important as braising was *simmering*, a slow,
prolonged process in which the food is subjected
sometimes for many hours, to a quiet, steady and con-
tinuous gentle heat – not sufficent to solidify, in meat, its
gelatinous constituents or to harden, in vegetables, their
cellulose fibres. The perfection of simmering depends on
the equability of the temperature, and that again on the

care which is taken to avoid sudden changes in the quality
of the heat that is applied to the foodstuffs. Generally an
iron pot was used that, after a preliminary boiling or
braising of the contents, was drawn aside to a cooler
position on the hearth and allowed to continue at the
same temperature for varying periods. Simmering was
especially effective with vegetable and meat stews. A
bredie, for instance, can never be exactly what it ought to
be unless it has been slowly simmered for several hours
to give all the constituents a proper chance to become
intimately blended into a composite whole that possesses
all the good qualities of its several ingredients.

Simmering, which is after all merely a variant of *stewing*
is economical and scientific. Properly done, it transforms
the foodstuff into its most appetising, palatable and
therefore nourishing form, developing, by this slow, steady
and prolonged action of moist heat chemical changes in
the food of whose nature and effect on digestion we still
do not know enough about to dogmatise.

Baking, roasting, frying, sauteeing and other methods
of direct application of heat did not differ in any degree
from those used by other cooks. Bread and cakes were
usually baked in brick or clay ovens – on some of the

methods farms in ant heaps excavated into suitable receptacles for the purpose — the heat being wood or brushwood and never coal or coke. Oven roasting, which is properly baking, was rarely used for meat, but very often for vegetables such as sweet potatoes, pumpkins and ordinary potatoes, and also for some made dishes such as *bobotie*, toad-in-the-hole, fruit and meat pies and of course all kinds of cakes and baked puddings.

Frying in deep fat was generally confined to town kitchens; on the farms and as a rule frying, or more properly sauteeing, was done in a shallow frying pan with just enough fat, lard or butter to give the necessary sharp moist heat to brown the substance fried. Batter was invariably used, but some of the old recipes distinctly state that bananas, pineapples, squashes, cucumbers and some other fruits and vegetables must not be fried in batter but by themselves — a directive that needs considerable skill and dexterity to carry out in such a way as to obtain a perfect result.

Steaming foodstuffs, either in their natural moisture, or in very little liquid of some other kind than their own juice (the *water-sootjie* business that is familiar enough to all cooks) was a popular method, particularly valuable when dealing with fish. It brought out the fine flavour of delicate foodstuffs, aided, when desired, by appropriate combinations of spices or herbs. A modification of this method, adopted in camp cookery, was to swathe the foodstuff in thick leaves, usually vine leaves or large dock leaves, in which they really simmered gently. Steaming needs a fairly low temperature, a gentle heat that percolates rather than concentrates its intensity on any particular section of the substance cooked.

In skilled hands it is one of the best methods of preparing food, but if the cook is inexperienced it usually produces something that is very much underdone, tough and insipid.

Much depends, in good cookery, on the preparation of the foodstuffs before they are subjected to one or other method of cooking. At the Cape beef has always been stringy, tough and tasteless; veal has been slightly better, though it has never reached the European or American standard of excellence. Both, therefore, require good larding and all old recipes are emphatic in their insistence that beef and game should be well larded. The larding was done, not with a needle, but by inserting good pork fat with the point of the knife an inch or two below the surface of the meat. Wild fowl were larded in the usual way and some kinds of fish, like the bonito, were larded with strips of bacon.

Larding has now died out of fashion, and is very rarely seen, although some old-fashioned cooks still use it, with the result that their dishes are far more savoury and succulent than anything that can be obtained in hotels or restaurants.

Preliminary *marinading* of meats was also popular; it is essential for *soesaties*, and for some kinds of *boboties*, although it is nowadays never used for the latter. It is also

28

useful in dealing with certain kinds of fish, especially fresh- **methods**
water fish. The marinade usually employed is a mixture of
natural wine and wine vinegar, in which has been steeped
various kinds of herbs, and sometimes wormwood (*wilde
als*) that is particularly admirable for game and waterfowl.

Old-time custom was to have two principal meals in the
day. There was no real breakfast. On arising in the early
morning, coffee and biscuits were taken. The first meal of
the day was about nine o'clock or later in the morning,
and was fairly substantial; the principal meal was after
noon and, later on, coffee and cake or preserves were
partaken of, with a supper in the evening.

In the middle of the eighteenth century, although the
chief meal was still at midday, fashionable circles provided a substantial collation between six and seven in the
afternoon and towards the end of the century some
families tended, under English influence, to concentrate
dinner in the evening as the chief meal of the day. During
the time of Lord Charles Somerset, when Government
House set the fashion, at least as far as Cape Town and its
immediate neighbourhood were concerned, the correct
dining hour was between five and six in the later afternoon, the dinners sometimes lasting till late in the night.

The Duke of Wellington, then a plain and unimportant
major, used to leave his lodgings at Maitland at four
o'clock to ride to the hospitable house at Newlands, where
he (as Cheap Jack has recorded the matter) was usually
"the only officer who hadn't to be helped to get on his
horse when he left", to attend the six o'clock dinner that
was reckoned the best in the Peninsula. The cook there
was a Coloured woman, the daughter of a Malay slave,
who had been trained by a Mozambique cook. Her pastries,
curries, bobooties, soesaties, and fish dishes were re-
nowned, and there is a legend that on occasion she was
invited to show her skill at Government House, which had
a white cook and stuck to French cookery.

Mrs Kindersley noted that Cape Town breakfasts were
even in her day, pretty substantial. That, however, was a
later innovation.

Fifty years ago all the good Cape Town hotels provided
a breakfast that today would be regarded as sumptuous
in the extreme. I have, as a boy, sat down at Haylett's
White House in the Strand at nine o'clock of a morning
to consume, not cereals and Melba toast (for these did not
figure on the bill of fare, though those who wanted it
could have old-fashioned oatmeal porridge served with
salt instead of sugar) but turmeric scones, *soesaties* with
fried bananas and fried eggs, long, much-spiced sausages
deliciously fried over wood coals, and a buffet of cold
game and fowl and gammon ham.

At Poole's in New Street — formerly Garden Street and
nowadays Queen Victoria Street — one could get partridge
pie, batter chops and yellow rice for breakfast, which indeed differed from the midday meal only in not having
soup on the bill. Dinner, at midday, was a fuller and
coarser matter. There was always soup, generally a full-
flavoured appetising thick soup, though sometimes, in

methods summer, a clear vegetable or herb soup was provided. Two kinds of fish came next, and thereafter stews, roasts, and vegetables, with a couple of sweets to follow. Wine was always served at this meal, in a carafe for the resident boarders, in bottles for the chance comers who paid for it, and it was generally a sound, wholesome natural wine. At dessert a sweet wine, usually fortified, was handed round, followed by coffee and preserves.

At private houses, both in town and on the farms, the ritual at dinner was much more elaborate and there, as is generally the case all over the world, one got far better and more skilfully prepared dishes than at any hotel. Some dishes were almost heirlooms; they could be tasted only at particular family houses and then only on special occasions. Others, more particularly those in which figured ingredients that could not be grown in gardens or cultivated but were obtained from the veld, could be tasted only on farms.

There was from the earliest times a good market at Cape Town, which persisted till the end of the past century when, like the beautiful foreshore between Mouille Point and Bantry Bay, it was sacrificed to the utilitarian gods that abhor whatever is beautiful and artistic. In that cool, inviting colonnade, one could get almost anything that one could think of for the kitchen — out-of-the-way herbs, tortoises and turtles; the tasty little "klip fish"; the aromatic berries that came from bushes growing on the edge of the Green Point Common lake; the succulent fennel roots that made such delicious preserve; the delightful, but rather vulgar, rose apples that some folk liked to mingle in their sweet dishes; the immense crayfish (the like of which one no longer sees, since Government has taken them under its protection and tried to teach us to call them crawfish); malagas eggs (more tasty than those of the penguin); and even that most delectable of all delicacies, the prepared skin of an adolescent porcupine.

In those circumstances it was comparatively easy to follow implicitly the directions in the old recipes, as there was no great difficulty in obtaining the necessary ingredients. Now it is sometimes impossible and generally very difficult to adhere faithfully to the directives.

Some travellers have complained that old Cape cookery was too greasy, too generous altogether in fats and titbits. The same charge has been laid against Italian cookery, German cookery and Creole cookery. It is true that certain dishes, notably the very fat Karroo-fed mutton when pot-roasted, are decidedly greasy, but a good cook can easily eliminate the oiliness. *Bredies* and stews insufficiently simmered and inexpertly prepared, may have a film of grease, but here too a good cook will know how to deal with it. Possibly the frequent use of wine in Cape cookery was an attempt to counteract the abundance of lard and sheep's tail fat so commonly used in farm cookery. Crisp frying, with adequate drainage when the fried portions are properly cooked, should also eliminate greasiness in most cases.

30

Chapter III

SPICES, HERBS AND FLAVOURINGS

THE art of making food palatable consists in skilfully improving the taste and quality of the foodstuffs by combining with their original flavour something that enhances and blends with it to bring out its full perfection. For that purpose we make use of various materials, generally those that possess a distinctive and sometimes a strong taste. Of these the most important are spices, herbs and extracts.

What are known as spices are, generally speaking, the mature or immature seeds of different species of plants, usually dried and prepared for the market. Only two kinds of spice, ginger and chillies, were grown in South Africa. From the earliest times most spices have been imported from the East Indies, nearly all in the ordinary commercial forms — though one kind, mace, was sometimes procured, privately, preserved in a thin syrup, a form in which it is no longer obtainable.

Of these various spices the chief were ginger, cinnamon and cassia, nutmeg and mace, pimento or allspice, cloves, black and white pepper, turmeric, chillies, saffron and garlic. Aromatic seeds such as poppy seed, mustard, celery seed, aniseed, caraway seed, cardamon seed, coriander seed, cumin seed, fennel seed and dill were also popular; but a few of the spicy seeds that figure in European recipes, such as fenugreek, capers and star aniseed and flavourings such as calamus, angelica, gentian, juniper berries and valerian are not ingredients in Cape cookery. A rare Oriental flavouring, zedoary, is mentioned in a few old recipes, but was never commonly used, and its neglect in modern days is no loss because it can easily be dispensed with, as can also that other

31

spices culinary absurdity, assafoetida, that is sometimes used in the preparation of Asiatic dishes.

Ginger is the underground stem of *zingiber officinale*, now locally grown to a large extent, although not in sufficient quantity to obviate importation. When fresh it is unpeeled and, like nearly all spices, contains starch and a volatile oil that gives to it its characteristic ginger taste, which is aromatic, biting and slightly sweet. The dried ginger, in which form it is usually sold on the market, is white or brown in colour and has lost its peel. It is more fibrous, less aromatic but a bit more pungent, can be powdered easily and retains its spicy flavour for a long time. It is indispensable for making curries, and is used as a flavouring in sweet dishes, condiments and some meat dishes and, to a slighter extent, in puddings and cakes.

Allspice, or *pimento*, is the fruit of *eugenia acris pimento*, a West Indian tree. It is exported in the dried form which, however, contains a large amount of the essential oil that gives it its characteristic clovelike flavour, known to chemists as *eugenol*. It is commonly used in all dishes in which cloves or pepper are likely to be admixed. In practice it is of little value when compared with these two spices and, as it easily loses its pungency when exposed to the air, it has never been popular in Cape cookery.

Cinnamon, on the other hand, is perhaps, next to pepper and nutmeg, the spice most commonly used at the Cape. Some old manuscript cookery books give precise and clear directions for distinguishing it from *cassia*, which to-day has almost totally supplanted it. Both are barks of an Oriental laurel tree ; cinnamon being derived from *cinnamonum zeylanicum*, and cassia from *C. cassia*. Both have a pleasant, cinnamon scent and a warm, aromatic and slightly sweet taste that are characteristics of cinnamon oil, a highly-volatile liquid whose chief constituent is cinnamic aldehyde.

Cassia is a coarser, more stringy bark, less fragrant but slightly sweeter than cinnamon, and it has a sharp pungency, that in some specimens is almost acrid and appears to be strengthened in the presence of sugar. For that reason there is a real difference in the quality of dishes prepared with cinnamon and that in which the cheaper and coarser cassia quills are used — a fact perfectly well known to old Cape cooks who were careful to use "the thinnest and finest Colombo cinnamon, soft enough to take the impress of one's nail". Such cinnamon was never bought in powder form, for it was known that cinnamon powder lent itself easily to adulteration ; it was always purchased as quills or "featherings", which were slightly cheaper — for Ceylon cinnamon was always a highly-priced spice on the market — and when it was wanted in powder form it was pounded in a mortar and sieved through a fine-meshed sieve. Generally, however, it was used whole, a small bit being broken off the quill and added to the dish.

For flavouring much less cinnamon had to be used than cassia but, as the latter was much the cheaper, it gra-

32

dually replaced the pure cinnamon and to-day, unfortunately, most cooks do not know the difference between the two. To the initiated, however, that difference is profound and may greatly influence the taste of a particular dish, especially when other flavourings are used at the same time. Cassia does not combine particularly well with some flavourings, whereas cinnamon blends blandly and kindly with most, even with the vulgar and pervasive vanilla.

Nutmeg and *mace*, although apparently so utterly different, are integral parts of one another, for the nutmeg is the seed of *myristica fragrans**; while mace is the beautiful red covering of that seed, which when dried is of a yellow or brownish red hue. It was formerly imported exclusively from Java, for its home is in the Moluccas, but the tree has for generations been cultivated in the West Indies and to-day the best nutmegs are said to come from Grenada. With cinnamon and pepper, nutmeg and mace may be said to be the most important spices employed in Cape cookery, for they figure in the oldest recipes and are still extensively used. One form in which they were formerly occasionally used, as a preserve of the ripe fruit in thin syrup, can no longer be obtained. This is a pity, for the syrup extracted much of the essential oil of both the covering and the kernel and served admirably as a concentrated flavouring for puddings and sweet dishes. Grated nutmeg goes with practically all steamed vegetables, while mace is incorporated in vegetable and meat stews. Both blend well with other flavourings and neither, when properly used, is overpowering.

The same cannot be said of *cloves* which are the dried unopened buds of *caryophyllus aromaticus*, another native tree of the Spice Islands. The commercial article has a pronounced aromatic scent and a strong, almost bitingly sharp, spicy taste. Zanzibar cloves are more mellow and less pungent. The aroma and taste they get from their essential oil, which is cousin-german to that contained in allspice. Cloves are used, somewhat arbitrarily, to flavour many sweet and unsweetened dishes and are an ingredient in all the standard recipes for the manufacture of Van der Hum liqueur. They should, however, be cautiously used and can easily be dispensed with in most cases, even when the recipe favours them. Their flavour blends indifferently well with other flavours and generally stifles the delicate taste of some vegetables and fruits.

Pepper, another typically-eastern spice of which there are several commercial varieties, technically called by the name of the particular town that exports them. In its official form it is the dried fruit capsule of *piper nigrum*, a climbing plant of the East Indian forests, now extensively cultivated. Black pepper is the fruit still complete in its dark, black husk; white pepper is the berry from which the dark outer covering has been removed by soaking and

---

*Various spices, indigenous and exotic, are grown. The Sante Fé nutmeg, pungent and coarse, is from *M. stobra*, which gives white mace. The Madagascar nutmeg is usually *M. acuminata*.

spices bruising it in warm water. The burning hot taste and aromatic pungent odour of both are from the essential oil contained in the whole berry and its covering. The so-called Long pepper, the berry of another species of *piper*, is less pungent and, like other kinds of pepper, comparatively rarely used in cookery. Substitutes for pepper, some containing the same essential oil and therefore to all intents and purposes equally fit for all purposes for which black pepper is employed, are found in all tropical countries. South Africa, too, possesses a wild pepper, the seeds of which on occasion serve as a make-shift.

Pepper has always been the chief and most important condiment spice; without it many dishes would lose the sharp, pleasingly warm taste that is a peculiarity of this flavouring. Practically all meat, and most vegetable dishes and soups, call for its addition, as it blends admirably with all. Even with sugar it may be made to agree, although it is not usually added to any sweet dish. The black variety is more pungent and more economical than the white, but the latter is required for dishes in which the intense black colour of the former is a disadvantage. The berries should always be added whole or, if desired in powder form, should be freshly ground in a pepper mill. Powdered pepper should always be preserved in closely-sealed jars, for the essential oil is volatile and easily dissipates, especially when the powder has been allowed to get wet.

When the East Indiaman *Haarlem*, with a cargo of spice on board, was wrecked on the shores of Table Bay some years before the settlement was started, the reek from the bags of pepper washed ashore lingered for many months in the vicinity and was even noted by some of the old travellers who visited the scene two years later.

Chillies, also known as red peppers, capsicum paprika, Cayenne pepper, pimiento, Mexican pepper, tabasco and hot pepper, are in Cape recipes invariably referred to as *rissies*, although sometimes the Malay word *lombok* is used and occasionally the Dutch *Spaansche peper*. They are, curiously enough, the fruit pods of a plant of the potato family and there are now many cultivated varieties, different from each other in their shape, colour and pungency. The immature pod is bright green, turning yellow or red when it ripens; its shape is elongated, oval or irregularly or smoothly round, sometimes as small as a cherry or a small pea pod, sometimes the size of a cucumber or a small squash. It may be used as a vegetable, in which case one of the larger and less pungent varieties – sweet peppers – must be chosen, but its main value in cookery lies in the peculiar flavour of the pod itself and, more especially, of the seeds. It is stated to contain no volatile oil, and all cooks know that the pods can be preserved in the open for many years without losing their intensely sharp, fiercely biting taste, a peculiarity that makes its dust most irritating to the eyes and nostrils of anyone handling it.

Whatever it is that imparts this extraordinarily sharp, stimulating quality to chillies, also imbues them with

34

distinctively individual merits that have long been appreciated and valued by South African cooks, who use them to an extent and in ways that are characteristic of much of their best cookery. Indeed, the test of the excellence of some South African soups and *bredies* is the manner in which the chilli flavour has been made to blend with, enhance, and modify that of the other ingredients. Great skill and experience are needed in using this spice; it is so powerful, sharp and acrid that it cannot possibly be made to harmonise with some dishes, but it is also so stimulating, so valuable as a contrasting flavour, and so delicious when properly used, that other dishes, without it, are insipid and altogether lack distincion.

While care is necessary in the use of all spices, none will repay patient and meticulous study and experiment better than chillies. Although there are probably more than 50 varieties in cultivation, only one – the ordinary small, attenuated, intensely sharp-tasting herb-garden variety that grows on a little bush half a foot high and flowers and fruits all the year round – need be stocked for kitchen use, and it does not greatly matter whether its pods are fresh or dried. When its full strength is required, the whole pod is used; when it is wished to have its flavour more mild, the seeds are first removed. The immature pod, which is bright green, is regarded as slightly milder than the full-grown, ripe, brilliantly red seed vessel.

Turmeric, like ginger, is the rootstock of an East Indian plant and is usually obtained only in powder form. I have seen it growing in old gardens at the Cape, but have never heard of the fresh rootstock being used in a Cape kitchen, although formerly the dried, or partly-dried, root was easily bought on the vegetable market. Its Dutch name, *kurkumana wortel*, is no longer used, having been replaced by the old term *borrie* that is used in the first recipes. It has a slightly bitter, and not a very pronounced aromatic taste, caused by a mild volatile oil. It contains much starch, and a colouring extractive that imparts a bright yellow tint to cellulose and albumin. Nowadays it is chiefly used in curries and in yellow rice dishes.

Saffron always has been the most expensive spice on the market and has, in consequence, been so much adulterated that most cooks have managed to do without it. It is, however, an extremely valuable spice, with a distinctive, individual flavour – slightly bitter, moderately pungent, and exceedingly penetrating – so that a very little goes a very long way in cookery. It readily gives up its bright yellow-red colouring matter, which is soluble in water and wine, and can be used to colour soups and sweet dishes. Real saffron is the dried stigma of the crocus, which is carefully plucked out when the flower is beginning to fade, spread on muslin and sun-dried. When dry, only the finest red stigmas are collected and sold by the ounce or gramme. They were usually retailed to cooks by the pennyweight.

Today there is almost no real saffron to be obtained; what passes for it is a substitute, the florets of a composite American plant, with a much less aromatic taste and a

spices more yellow colour. It does very well for cakes and biscuits, but hardly can replace the real article in soups and fish dishes.

Garlic is extensively grown at the Cape and no longer imported, so that it is possible to get fresh bulbs. The commercial powder, which is a mixture of pounded bulb, starch and salt, never need be used. As a flavouring, garlic has always been popular with Cape cooks, who used it more sparingly than their Oriental contemporaries, and combined it, perhaps more skilfully, with other spices. They sometimes used a native garlic (*tulbaghia sp*) a common garden plant with lilac blue flowers, whose leaves are excellent as a substitute for true garlic but whose bulbs are much too strongly aromatic for culinary use.

The Cape cook relied greatly, so far as his spicy seeds were concerned, on *coriander* seed, that was formerly extensively imported from Asia but is now home-grown. It is derived from a plant of the carrot family, which has a pretty, feathery white flower and small, ridged seeds that are supposed to resemble a bedbug. To this fancied resemblance the plant owes its name, which is from the Greek for one of these disgusting little goggas. The seed, however, is far from disgusting. It has a clean aromatic odour and taste and imparts an agreeable flavour to all meats and starches, while it can be preserved for some time without losing its good qualities. A little bruising generally brings out these much better.

Mustard seed is too well-known to need comment; it is now always used in its powdered, commercial form. A very little of it may on occasion be advantageous in a dish, but it contains so outrageously active an intestinal irritant (known to chemists as isothiocyanate of allyl) that it should be employed with the utmost caution. All the piquancy that it is supposed, in the advertisements, to give to whatever we eat, can be more healthily and artistically given by other condiments.

Poppy seed, on the other hand, has no deleterious qualities. They are slightly nutty in taste and are prescribed in some old recipes for adorning cakes. They contain no opium, and the good lady traveller who states that she "fell asleep too readily after eating of the poppy-cakes" somewhere in Strand Street, was most certainly drawing on a saltatory imagination.

Cardamon, *celery* and *dill* seed are sparingly used in their current commercial forms. *Fennel seed* is less commonly used than fennel leaves or, in some old-fashioned kitchens, the root of the plant. *Caraway*, *aniseed* and *cumin* are much more popular.

They may be said to be the chief spice seeds in daily use and all three have distinctive odours and tastes, though when subjected to heat there is not much difference between any two of them. Aniseed, perhaps, imparts more of its peculiar flavour to farinaceous dishes than does either cumin or caraway, while the two latter also give a less pronounced flavour and taste to any liquid in which they are steeped or boiled. The so-called

36

star aniseed is not a seed at all, and although it is often **spices** used in Oriental cookery, I have never seen it mentioned in any authentic Cape recipe, though it has lately made its appearance (obviously derived from second-hand American sources) in popular cookery hints by someone who apparently has vague ideas of what kind of spice it is.

More than on spicy seeds the Cape cook relies on flavouring extracts that he obtains from fresh herbs and leaves. Formerly every house that had a garden, had a corner of it reserved for the growing of pot and kitchen herbs. How varied and extensive these collections were

in some cases is exemplified by the jottings, in one manuscript book, of a Cape lady writing at the beginning of the last century:

In the little garden there are now: mint, thyme, mignonette, Spanish peppers, rosemary, endive, wild garlic, pepperroot, nasturtiums, tarragon, mountain sage, marjoram, celery, anise, sorrel, and scented verbena . . . the bean-herb (savory) has died and so has the balsam herb (basil) which cannot be replaced . . .

All these are still used and all are referred to, somewhere or other, in old Cape recipes; but some, like savory and basil, tarragon and pepperroot, sweet thyme and catmint, are now exceedingly scarce and hardly to be obtained even from the nurserymen. As most of them are well known, we need say little about them here, but sorrel and scented verbena are fully worth an annotation.

Sorrel is of two kinds. There is the common or garden sorrel, also known as French or Belgian sorrel, that is easily cultivated in the garden and is the sort that is mentioned in all cookery books. The other kind is the indigenous "Cape sorrel", to pick which the mariners landed on the Peninsula nearly a hundred years before Van Riebeeck established his refreshment station here. It is a true *oxalis,* flourishes extensively all through winter, spring and early summer, and sometimes makes splendid splashes of chrome yellow on the hills.

Its history cannot be told here, for it is too long and intricate a tale. In the kitchen it serves to soften and im-

spices prove nearly all vegetable stews; makes an excellent soup; and may even be served up as vegetable puree or in its uncooked form added to a vegetable salad. It is pleasantly sub-acid and probably (if that is of the least interest to any cook) has quite a considerable amount of vitamin, but for all that it is an excellent food adjunct without which Cape cookery would not be what it should be.

Scented verbena (and to some extent also the various sweet-scented indigenous pelargoniums) may be used for flavouring, for blending with other herbs in vegetable and meat stews and in soups, and as addition to sweet drinks. Their essential oils are soft and fragrant, combine admirably with various spices, and are perfectly harmless.

So too are *laurel leaves*, the foliage of the sweet bay tree (*laurus nobilis*), native to southern Europe but fairly common in Cape gardens. The leaves have a characteristic scent of oil of laurel and an aromatic, slightly bitter and astringent taste. They are used alone or in combination with other flavouring materials, generally in cold dishes, such as brawns and marinated fish or meats. Some caution must be observed in their use, for a decoction of the leaves is decidedly poisonous. Probably for this reason they are usually replaced in Cape cooking recipes by *lemon leaves*, whose flavour, odour and taste are very similar and whose use is devoid of danger.

There are several other kinds of leaves, such as those of the peach, the pittosporum, and orange or tangerine, that are used for flavouring, while young fig leaves are sometimes added to soups or stews to give a bright green colour.

In a country with such vast botanical wealth it is not surprising to find many different kinds of wild plants that can with advantage be added to the already long list of spices and flavourings. Some of these will be mentioned when we discuss camp cooking, but most of them have not yet been fairly tried. Much remains to be done in this wide and fallow field, where the ingenuity and artistry of the expert cook may find scope for unlimited combination and experiment. One need refer only to one of the most fragrant and distinctive South African seeds, that of the *gethyllis*, whose pods are now used solely to scent domestic linen, but whose possibilities as a food flavouring appear to be vast.

There remains one other flavouring that does not fall into any of the categories that have so far been dealt with. This is *tamarind*, the pasty dried fruit of an Indian tree that was at one period deemed indispensable in the preparation of many Cape dishes, particularly curries. For several years good tamarind has been practically unobtainable; now it is again on the market, and it should be used wherever it is prescribed in the recipes. An infusion of the fruit is more aromatic and spicier than *vinegar*, which in modern days has almost supplanted it. It need scarcely be said that the vinegar used in Cape cookery is always good wine vinegar; wood or malt vinegar is never used by any cook who has the slightest respect for his art or his dishes.

Extracts of herbs or spices in vinegar are useful to have at hand when the fresh or dried flavourings cannot be obtained.

In conclusion I may briefly refer to one or two other flavourings that are mentioned in many recipes. One is *tangerine peel* (*naartjieskil*) the dried rind of the tangerine or mandarin orange commonly found throughout South Africa. It is used in small pieces, for it is a strong and distinctive flavouring, and nearly always for sweet dishes. Lemon and orange, citron and cumquat peel or zests are also used according to taste; each has its own, slightly different, taste and flavour, and all are pleasingly and warmly aromatic.

Several kinds of nuts are also favoured. Among these pistachio, almonds, both the sweet and the bitter kind, peach and apricot kernels, and pine kernels — all ingredients in old recipes. Of these pistachio alone is imported; all the others are home-grown.

For colouring, powdered ochre, saffron and turmeric were relied on although much use was made of caramel, molasses and *moskonfyt*. Perfumes were used in the early eighteenth century, but fell into disfavour. Their place was taken by the essential oils of almonds and lemon. Rose water and orange flower-water are mentioned in some recipes; musk in one only.

Chapter IV

SOUPS

Following the west-European custom of starting the principal meal with a soup course, Cape colonists did not know, or if they knew did not use, *hors d'oeuvres* as a preparatory relish at lunch or dinner. *Vorspeise* of this sort were introduced from Russia and the Scandinavian countries, and recipes for their preparation are not found in the old colonial manuscript books. Soups, on the other hand, were always popular, and the humblest kitchen relied on a good soup to start a meal. The result was that most of the Cape soups were considered as an integral part of the meal, rather than as a relish to stimulate appetite. They were almost without exception highly-nutritious, satisfying concoctions, well flavoured and rich — varying in consistency from the thin liquid vegetable consommés to the almost porridge-like consistency of the heavy purees and game soups with their added thickening of farinacious material.

They were usually carefully prepared, for to a large extent the skill of the cook was tested by the soup. Artificial colouring was rarely used; when necessary, burnt sugar or a brown roux, the preparation of which differed in no way from that prescribed in printed cookery books, was used. For a red colour, beetroot leaves; for green, spinach or fig leaves; and for a bright yellow, turmeric or curry powder could be employed. In one recipe for fish soup, saffron is mentioned, which gives a pale apricot tint. For the richer soups a zest of egg yolks beaten up with a glass of wine and a grating of nutmeg, was nearly always prescribed. It was placed in the soup tureen and the boiling soup was poured on it immediately before serving.

With such rich soups, snippets of bread, fried in fat, were handed round; with curry soups, white rice, cooked dry, was served in some households; and salt dried fish, *bokkoms* or "Indian duck" as old East Indians preferred to call it, in others.

The soup was ladled out by the hostess into deep china or earthenware plates, and handed round to the guests, each being served with a liberal portion. It was not the custom to hand round cream or any made-up condiment with the soup; all spice or flavouring that was necessary was put in before it reached the table. I have known a guest's name deleted from his hostess' dining list because he had added salt and pepper to his soup, thereby inferentially questioning the cook's skill.

Nowadays we are not so strong minded, and it is not uncommon to see some "bright young thing" lighting a cigarette at table between the soup and the fish course, unwithered by an appositely-scathing remark from her hostess.

The basic constituent of most soups is a meat extract in water, such as a beef bouillon, a consommé in the manufacture of which two different kinds of meat, usually beef and mutton, have been used, and a veal consommé. When these are used instead of water, the soup is of course richer and contains an additional amount of nourishment. It is seldom, however, that the old recipes prescribe these basic liquids. They usually direct that, if meat of any kind is to be used, such meat should be boiled with the other ingredients. In a number of soups no meat whatever is used, and the substitutes for a meat extract are then milk, wine, beer, fruit juice, and especially coconut milk.

The last is prepared by scraping the flesh of a ripe coconut, adding to it the original fluid contained in the nut, and then pouring boiling water over it. As soon as the water cools, the mixture is compressed and all the moisture forced out. Such coconut milk is a thin, whitish-grey fluid slightly sweet and glutinous to the taste; it serves admirably as a diluent and has many other uses in Cape cookery. What remains after the moisture has been extracted, the dry, white scrapings, still has a certain amount of flavour and considerable food value, and may be used for puddings, cakes and some entrees.

It is not my intention to write down the recipes for the several hundred different kinds of soups. All are to be found in printed cookery books, and most of them are variations of directives that appear in the oldest. There are, however, recipes that have been modified at the Cape and a few others that, on account of the purely local character of some of their constituents, may be said to be peculiar to South Africa. In a postwar Afrikaans cookery

41

soups book, 110 kinds of soups are described ; of these probably a fourth may claim to differ in some way from similar kinds enumerated in European cookery books published before the middle of the last century. There is ample scope for the ingenuity of the South African cook to concoct new kinds by slightly modifying these age-old recipes and by blending the ingredients with some of the distinctive local herbs and flavourings.

One of the best soups of which mention is made in the older recipes was undoubtedly developed on the lines laid down by the wandering demobbed soldier in Grimm's folk-tale. When the first mariners walked on the shores of Table Bay, they found round them almost a meadowland sprinkled with all sorts of edible herbs that to sailormen, yearning for fresh vegetables to counteract the persistent tendency to scurvy that endangered all long voyages, promised immediate relief. It was easy enough to gather armloads of these greens, boil them in the caboose with the addition of scraps of salt pork, consume the resultant liquid as a health-giving soup, and serve up the remaining mess as a vegetable stew.

Later there was opportunity to be more selective, dis-criminating and artistic, and the varieties of this vegetable soup show a progressive aptitude for studying flavour and blending tastes. A comprehensive synopsis of these different recipes is afforded by the following directions in one of the oldest manuscripts.

Garden Soup. Take of thyme, marjoram, young leaves of the beetroot, sorrel, dock and lettuce enough for your purpose ; chop up a handful of green beans, a couple of young onions, with their leaves, a slice of green pumpkin, a couple of soft, young turnips, and a medium-sized green chilli. Put all into the soup pot and cover with cold water. Bring to the boil and skim ; then let slowly simmer for four hours, adding lukewarm water to make up for what evaporates. Add a bit of mace, a few slices of green ginger and a few pepper corns, and allow to simmer for half an hour longer. Strain through muslin and serve after salting.

The result should be a thin, reddish-brown liquid, deliciously and pungently aromatic which, if it is too sharp for ordinary tastes, may be diluted advantageously with a dash of cream, a few tablespoons of coconut milk, or a glass of wine. Almost anything in the garden may be used, in preparing this soup ; in fact, the more varied the mixture of herbs and vegetables is, the better will be the result. What remains after straining may be mashed with butter and a dash of wine into a tasty puree, after removing the remnants of the mace, pepper corns, and chilli.

The soup is as good if it is served cold after a short spell in the refrigerator.

Crayfish soup. Select for this the female of the species, which you will know by the double toed claw or, better still, by the hispidity under the tail.

Select, if you can get them, living crayfish, dark brown

and crawling, and eschew the cardinal-coloured, commercially-boiled ones that lack all delicacy, whose flesh
is sodden and stringy. Proceed according to the old-
fashioned recipe, compiled by cooks who knew how to
get the best out of these tasty crustaceans.

Take two young carrots, two onions, two shallots, two
lemon leaves, a teaspoonful of thyme, a clove of garlic
bruised, a few scented verbena leaves; a slither of lemon
rind, a slice of fat bacon, and half a pound of raw ham;
chop these fine, and simmer lightly with butter. Season
with pepper and salt; pour over a bottle of wine and let
the whole boil up. Boil your crayfish in this mirepoix, and
let it cool down in it when cooked.

Now take out your crayfish, and remove from it all the
flesh, especially the soft white and green substance
found under the carapace, and the meat from the larger
claws. Crush the remains of the crayfish in a mortar, and
put it back, together with part of the tail flesh, in the
mirepoix, to which you add a few cups of good fish or
mutton stock, and let it slowly simmer for a couple of
hours. Strain, and set the liquor aside for the moment.

Pound the flesh, together with the coral and green
meat, in a mortar with some butter, a morsel of mace, and a
pinch of ginger powder, and add it to the liquor; simmer
slowly taking care that no lumps are formed and add,
finally, half a cupful of boiled rice, and some of the tail
flesh cut into dice.

Beat up a couple of egg yolks in the soup tureen with a
glassful of sherry, pour in the soup, and serve immediately
with croutons of fried bread.

A crayfish *bisque*, prepared in this way, is a rich, delicately-flavoured soup, far different from that ordinarily
made from commercially-boiled crayfish or cold-storage
tails. Some folk put in a handful of green seaweed; others
add cream, which makes a smoother but heavier soup.
By adding curry or turmeric powder it becomes a crayfish
mulligatawny; with tomatoes and potatoes mixed in it, it
becomes a crayfish *chowder*. Experts garnish it with
marble-sized dumplings made from the soft carapace
flesh and the coral, mixed with egg white and boiled in
the soup.

The test of its excellence is the exquisite flavour given to
it by the soft parts found under the carapace, which is
usually lost when the tail flesh alone is used. Old recipes
warn against the reputedly dangerous intestinal tract in
the animal which, as a matter of fact, easily comes away
and has really no poisonous properties.

Fish soup, made from the firmer varieties such as
bonito or yellow tail and Cape salmon (geelbek) is prepared in much the same way, by first making a strong and
well-flavoured fish stock from the bones, adding portions
of the fish (sometimes first lightly fried in butter or lard)
and pouring the boiling liquid over a zest of beaten yolk
of egg mixed with cream and a glass of wine.

A curry fish soup, and one in which saffron is used, are

43

soups merely variations of this method which lends itself to innumerable modifications.

A fish chowder and a *bouillabaise* need for their proper preparation a variety of fish, cooked in a rich stock with the addition of potatoes and tomatoes, ochra or green beans for the one, and saffron, garlic and green ginger for the other. All fish soups are improved by boiling some green seaweed with them; few by the addition of chillies (a notable exception is curried fish, which is eaten cold). They are thickened, if desired, by rice flour, tapioca or maizena, and can be made extravagantly glutinous by ochra or sea weed.

Bean soup. There are many kinds of beans and all, when dried, make excellent soup — though some, like the small black-and-white sort, have a peculiar flavour. Perhaps the best of all is the large, almost inch long and proportionately broad, beautifully marbled *governor's beans* that could formerly be obtained cheaply but nowadays are quite costly.

As an example of the general recipe for bean soup the following recipe for a dish made from *heereboontjies*, as these big marbled beans were formerly called, will serve:

Soak two pounds of beans in cold water; peel them, rejecting all that float. Braise some sliced onions, a small green chilli, a slice of green ginger, and some green herbs in butter or fat; pour over cold water, add the beans, a slice of fat pork and a mutton bone and let the whole simmer carefully for several hours, stirring the pot frequently and skimming carefully to remove the fat. Pour through the tammy, and separate the beans, keeping a few of them whole; mash the rest and return to the liquid. Salt and pepper to taste and boil for a quarter of an hour; add a glass of wine and serve.

It should be a smooth, white, moderately-thick soup, which some people enrich by adding cream and egg yolk, although it requires neither, being by itself a nourishing and exceedingly palatable broth.

All dried pulses may be used for soup in the same way. A strong, harshly-flavoured dried pea, lentil or bean soup is made with salt pork and is served garnished with croutons of fried bread. This is a favourite caboose dish and was formerly, under the name of *snert*, exceedingly popular; but it is perhaps too powerfully flavoured for ordinary palates. A thin bean consommé, made from bouillon in which dried beans have been boiled, is a delicately-flavoured soup that fulfils all the requirements for a preliminary dinner relish. For garnish, the whole beans that have escaped the mashing process, are to be used. Some recipes prescribe a sprinkling of fennel leaves, and all white soups are supposed to be improved by the addition of grated nutmeg.

Limpet soup. Limpets, periwinkles and mussels were formerly easily obtainable; they flourished within hand grasp in the waters washing the shores of Table Bay. Now one must go far afield to get specimens that are not

sullied by sewage, and as they are no longer sold on the
fish market, one must gather them laboriously with
personal effort. Limpet soup, as made by the old Malay
cooks, was a distinctive and highly fragrant, appetising
dish, and was prepared as follows:

Collect as many limpets off the rocks as your backache
allows you; put them in a bucket of fresh water and clean
them as well as you are able to. A coarse scrubbing brush
helps, but do not be too pernickety so long as you get
rid of most of the sand. Put them into a mortar and crush
their shells and then, without washing them again, place
them in the soup pot, with some sliced onions, a garlic
clove, a handful of green sea weed and some pepper
corns; it does not matter if you are slightly extravagant
with the pepper. Boil them up, and then let them simmer
gently for a couple of hours. Strain through cloth, and put
the liquid back into the pot. Add some burnt roux or
burnt sugar mixed with a little flour, some salt (very little is
needed) and, if you like, a tablespoonful of ketchup or
Worcester sauce, and boil up once more. Finally add a
couple of glasses of sherry and serve.

Mussel soup can be made in the same way, but a far
better method for mussels, especially the white variety,
is to stew them lightly with herbs and butter and then
pass them through a mincing machine or pound them in
a mortar before simmering them in a good fish stock or
bouillon. This mussel soup really needs no thickening,
but is improved by adding cream. Another delicious soup
is *klipkous soup* which is made from the flesh of the
large pearl mussel (*haliotis capensis*) after it has been
prepared for the table (see the recipe for pearl mussel).
Into a rich fish stock, adequately spiced and herb flavoured, the pounded and cooked flesh is stirred slowly, to
avoid forming lumps, and then simmered gently for a
quarter of an hour.

Some people add saffron to this soup, but that is a
mistake, for the flavour of the *haliotis* is distinctive,
delicate, and easily overpowered. Blending must therefore
be skilfully done, and no soup needs more tasting on the
part of the cook than this. When properly made, it should
be smooth, greyish-white in colour, fragrant and full of
the rich suavity of taste that is the hall mark of the shell-
fish itself. I have never been quite satisfied that the
addition of wine or cream add greatly to either its taste
or its subtleness, but most recipes advise one or other of
these adjuncts.

Turtle soup was well known to Cape cooks and at one
time dried turtle, and on occasion fresh bits of the creature,
were easily procurable at the fish market; but now it is a
rarity and proportionately expensive. The manner in which
it was prepared differed in no way from that prescribed in
the printed manuals on cookery and ranged from Careme's
elaborate recipe to the simpler ones in which far fewer
ingredients were used. Cape cooks specified a conglome-

soups ration of spices – the more, apparently, the better – and favoured large pieces of the flesh, so succulently fat, for garnishing.

Tortoise soup, made from the native tortoise that prowled all over the Cape Peninsula and is now protected inside and outside its borders, was esteemed a particularly efficacious tonic. The water tortoise, that is admirable eating, was rarely used for soup, probably because of its obnoxious odour. To make the soup the tortoise was killed, thoroughly scrubbed in warm water, and then boiled in slightly salted water to which herbs and spices had been added according to taste. The boiling lasting until the animal had practically fallen to pieces. The liquid was then strained off and, for medicinal purposes, was left to get jellied. If wanted immediately, it was thickened with some tapioca. A little lemon juice and a cupful of wine were added and it was sent to table garnished with titbits of the flesh, preferably also of the liver, previously fried in butter.

It made an admirable clear soup, with a distinctive but not too strong flavour, and was quite equal to the clear turtle soup made from dried meat.

Another soup that was reputed to possess medicinal value was *fish-roe soup*, of which the method was a variation of one of the oldest recipes in existence, and one of these that owed more to Occidental than to Eastern tradition:

Soak the roes in water and remove all membrane. Simmer them slowly in a mirepoix made with vinegar, onions, green ginger and herbs; take them out and cut them up into small pieces, which you then place, with a cupful of green peas, in some good bouillon; simmer gently; add a glassful of white wine, grate nutmeg over (some cooks prefer powdered fennel) and serve with toasted bread.

Game soup was generally made from several kinds of game and wild fowl, usually with the addition of fat pork. It was always heavily-herbed and spiced, thickened with brown roux, and strengthened by the addition of a moderately sweet wine. Sometimes it was preferred slightly sour, in which case the brown roux was mixed with vinegar or lemon juice.

Sour cream was never served with it; indeed, sour cream is rarely mentioned in the old recipes, and is even today scarcely ever used. Which is a pity, for with clear vegetable soups, especially those like garden soup, its addition is often an improvement.

Other meat soups, such as *veal soup, oxtail soup, calfshead soup, calfsfoot soup, tripe soup, liver soup* and *kidney soup*, were made in accordance with the usual recipes given in printed cookery books, though here and there one notices slight modifications that individual cooks have made. These are not always improvements on the orthodox directives. With meat soups, dumplings or small meat balls were sometimes served.

An interesting paraphrase of the old fashioned *blanc-*

46

Cream chicken soup. Lightly brown a cooking fowl in fat or butter; simmer it in bouillon with a couple of sliced onions, a couple of carrots and a bunch of mixed herbs. When tender, take out and remove all the white flesh; replace the carcass and brown flesh in the soup pot and allow it to simmer. Pound the white flesh in a mortar with half a pound of cooked rice, a lump of butter, and a morsel of mace; add this to the soup pot and allow to simmer slowly for half an hour; now add a cupful of coconut milk (some recipes prescribe almond milk) and let it come to the boil. Pour through a tammy, and then into the soup tureen in which you have mixed a couple of egg yolks with a cupful of cream. Grate nutmeg over and serve immediately.

This soup should be a fairly thick puree, smooth and without lumps. It needs no pepper, but salt should be added, though the old recipe which I quote here does

not mention it, probably because salted butter was used for browning the chicken. The taste should be delicate and would be spoiled by the addition of wine.

Mulligatawny soup. There are many recipes for this, which is essentially an eastern soup. It may be a thin clear curry-spiced consomme, or it may be a thick *potage*. The best cooks used to make it with fresh spices, but today it is far more easy to use any good curry powder. The basis of the soup is a rich, strong double stock, made principally of chicken meat with a small amount of beef added to give "body". One recipe runs as follows:

Cut into pieces a good sized fowl and lightly brown in fat; place them in the soup pot with four peeled and sliced mealy apples, four onions, a clove of garlic, previously bruised and slightly browned in butter, the bone from a roast leg of mutton from which most of the meat has been removed and, tied in a bit of muslin, a sprig of mint, thyme, and marjoram, a bruised red chilli, some pepper corns and a morsel of mace. Allow to come to the boil and simmer slowly for a couple of hours.

Remove the mutton bone and the herbs. Take an ounce of tamarind, previously steeped in water; pound it in a

soups mortar with the water in which it has been steeped; pour through a wire sieve, and mix the liquid smoothly with two tablespoonsful of curry powder with an equal amount of fine rice flour. Let the soup come to the boil and stir in this mixture, taking care to allow no lumps to form; continue stirring for some minutes while it boils. Pour through a sieve or tammy, adding salt; put some of the chicken meat, boned, into the soup tureen; pour over a glass of white wine, add the soup and serve at once, handing round hot boiled rice or, if you like, pounded dried fish with it.

In all meat soups and generally, too, in others, it is significant that the old recipes prefer that salt should be added at the last moment. This is correct, provided it is permitted to dissolve completely and become intimately mixed with the liquid. Its addition at an earlier stage may harden some ingredients and undoubtedly does interfere with the proper blending of some of the spices and herbs, perhaps because of the chemical action of the salt solution on the essential oils.

Of the vegetable soups that have a particular local significance there are some that are prepared from plants that are indigenous, but their preparation differs in no way from that of any other vegetable soup. Their basis is a good stock; it may be a prepared meat stock, a vegetable stock, or a composite stock made by boiling the vegetable itself with meat and bones or with another vegetable. If the vegetable is mashed in the soup, it becomes a thick puree; if portions alone are retained and the soup consists merely of the juice and extractives from the vegetables used, it is a thin, clear or clouded consomme. Sometimes the vegetables are put into the cold bouillon or water without any preparation; sometimes they are first lightly braised in butter or fat, or dusted with flour before the water is poured on them. In all vegetable soups herbs and spices figure, according to most South African formularies.

As examples of vegetable soups made from ingredients peculiar to South Africa the following may be cited.

Uintjie soup. Uintjies are the edible corms of certain species of an iris (*morea edule*) or of an oxalis (*oxalis lupinifolia*), both of which are in season in the early spring (July to September). The corms are first boiled in salted water, peeled, and then made into a soup precisely in the manner in which governor's beans are done. The taste is like that of chestnuts. The soup, when well prepared, is a rich, creamy white, nourishing and highly appetising.

Water hawthorn soup is made from a puree of the buds of the wild water hawthorn or water-uintjie (*aponogeton sp*) a common plant that grows on most inland ponds and shallow river reaches, and is in season in winter and spring.

Sorrel soup is made from the leaves of the wild, yellow flowered sorrel (*oxalis pes-caprae*), that may be gathered almost all the year round. *Wild cabbage soup* is made from the buds of a veld plant, an *anthericum*, that blossoms in

48

winter. In addition the buds of one kind of aloe, the white **soups** part of the thick leaves of a river plant (*prionum palmita*), the fronds of the bracken fern, and one or two kinds of sea weed provide ingredients for making soups that have a distinctive taste. Their preparation is simple like that of spinach or lettuce soup. The cook prepares a good stock, in which the vegetable is boiled, with or without the addition of spices. In most cases, where the veld plant has a particularly delicate flavour, spices should be used with caution to enhance and not overpower the distinctive flavour of the principal ingredient.

Cape cooks also favoured sweet soups, which in winter were usually served hot and in summer chilled. Most of them are wine soups; a few, like *loquat soup*, are fruit soups, and are simply a mixture of fruit juices with a wine stock, thickened with rice flour or cream, or in some cases with coconut milk. The oldest recipe for a wine soup in my collection is the following:

Wine soup (wynsoep). Boil four cups of unskimmed milk with a morsel of tangerine peel, a blade of mace, a slither of cinnamon and four allspice; stir in a tablespoonful of butter and two ounces of candy sugar. Boil separately three pints of red wine with a slice of green ginger and a pinch of aniseed, and as soon as it comes to the boil stir it in the boiling milk; add a pinch of salt; let it stand where it remains hot, but do not let it boil again. Beat up two fresh eggs in the soup tureen and pour the hot soup over them, beating continuously so that the eggs are thoroughly mixed with the soup. Grate nutmeg over, and serve with thin, sweet biscuits.

Another simpler and equally good recipe: Cut a lemon in slices and sprinkle it with powdered candy sugar. Take a cupful of white breadcrumbs, and toss them in a pan in melted butter until they have absorbed it all; place the slices of lemon on top and let them remain there while the pan is kept hot on the side of the stove. Boil up four cups of a good red or white wine with some candy sugar, a feathering of cinnamon, and a couple of cloves. Put the soaked crumbs and the slices of lemon in the soup tureen and pour over them the boiling wine. Put on the cover and let the soup stand for ten minutes; stir, grate some nutmeg on the top and serve with toasted bread.

Both kinds may be served cold, if desired. Wine and beer soups are sometimes thickened with sago or tapioca and garnished with raisins or preserved citron. A peculiarly fragrant — and it must be added, rather an insipid — wine soup is made with rose apples.

A few more recipes:

Green mielie soup. Cut the mielies from the cob, and cook them in a mixture of four parts water and one part white wine, to which you have added a bunch of herbs, a blade of mace and some pepper corns. When tender, take out the corn, mash it, and return it to the soup pot,

49

soups with a cupful of strong meat stock, properly salted. Let it simmer for half an hour; then stir in a teaspoonful of candy sugar and serve.

Sometimes this soup is thickened by adding a white sauce, but it is better without that addition.

Garlic soup. Braise some sliced onions in butter with a clove of bruised garlic and a small bit of onion leaf. Add 24 cloves and as many black pepper corns. Mix a tea-spoonful of good curry powder in half a cupful of tamarind water, and stir this into the braise; add ten cups of good stock (or of coconut milk) and let it boil; then add a pound of ripe tomatoes, peeled and cut into quarters, a bay leaf and a lemon leaf, and salt to taste. Let it simmer slowly; pour through a coarse sieve and serve with fried bread.

The recipe states: "This soup has a decidedly sharp taste, and many prefer to dilute it with sour cream."

Blood soup. Take the fresh blood of a fowl and mix it with sifted flour, vinegar, powdered white pepper and salt. Stir this mixture slowly into a boiling chicken stock. Serve with meat balls made by mixing finely-minced chicken meat with white of egg, spiced with mace, ginger powder and salt and pepper and boiled in the soup.

Bread Soup. Take slices of stale white bread; remove the crust and boil the slices in a good, well-spiced, chicken consomme. Take out and press through a wire sieve; mix with butter, grated nutmeg, salt and white pepper; return to the soup pot and let it boil, stirring care-fully to prevent lumping. Serve in plates and garnish each plate with a poached egg dusted with nutmeg.

A similar soup is made with onions and bread, and is one of the variations of the many *onion soup* recipes.

Pawpaw soup. This is made from green pawpaws, boiled in a highly-spiced and herb-flavoured bouillon, mashed and then passed through the tammy. A glass of sherry improves it, and it is one of the few vegetable soups in which a suspicion of chilli enhances the flavour. An equally smooth soup can be made from avocado pears.

Chapter V

FISH AND SEA FOOD

THE seas that wash the African continent are extraordinarily rich in things that are not merely edible but appetisingly eatable. They range from algae or sea weed to the many varieties of fish, shell fish and other invertebrates, and cetaceans that are really salt water mammals and should, properly speaking, be considered in the following chapter which deals with meat.

There was a time when the Cape Town fish market was the repository of practically all fish in season; when, on the little sandy cove at the bottom of Adderley Street, when the fishing boats came in one could cheaply buy them freshly caught; and when, at Kalk Bay, one could even get a bunch of mullets for the asking, so plentiful was the catch. The raucous horn of the fish cart was heard every morning in the centre and suburbs of the town; a large *snoek* changed owners for a modest four pennies; and an immense crayfish cost a penny. Today we have changed all that and fish, that can and should be among the cheapest of foodstuffs, is prodigiously dear, hardly ever fresh, and never in sufficient supply to meet the demand.

With some patience and a knowledge of local conditions, however, most of the different kinds can still be obtained when in season, though some of the best, like butterfish, klipfish, and klip sole, are rarely to be seen.

More than a 100 years ago, an enthusiastic district surgeon published a list of 40 different kinds of edible fish

51

fish to be obtained in the Cape Town fish market. His pamphlet is now a rare bit of Africana and contains some interesting particulars about the better known varieties. Among these are the following:

Banksteenbras (*palunolepis grandis. gunth*), Baardman (*umbrina capensis. pappe*), Bonito (*sarda sarda. Bloch*), Bontrok (*sargus cervinus lowe*), Bishop (*sparus sp.*), Dassie (*sargus rondeletti*), Daybreak or Dageraad (*pagrus laticeps*), Galjoen (*dipteron capensis*), Geelbek (*atractoscion aequideris*), Albacore or Yellowtail (*seriola lalandii*), Hottentot (*gymnocrolaphus curvidens gunth*), Leatherfish (*lichnia amia I*), Kabeljou (*sciaena holopelidota*), Katonkel (*scomberomorus commersonii*), Mackerel (*scomber colias*), Maasbanker (*trachurus trachurus*), Snoek (*thyrsites atun*), Red steenbras (*dentex rupestris*), White steenbras (*pagellus lithognatus*), Red stumpnose (*pagrus gibbiceps*), White stumpnose (*sparus globiceps*), Red Roman (*pagrus laticeps*), Stock fish, Klipfish, Haarder or Mullet, Springer, Butterfish, Pilchard, Skate, Sole, Klipsole, King Klipfish, Elf, Jacopiewer or Gurnard, Kalk or Chalk fish, and Silverfish.

Of these the sorts that are still easily obtainable in season are galjoen, geelbek, yellowtail, hottentot, kabeljou, mackerel, maasbanker, kingklip, snoek, the two kinds of steenbras, red and white, red and white stumpnose, red roman, stockfish, haarder, sole, skate, silverfish, elf and gurnard. Katonkel, a delicious game fish, is rarely seen though it is more common on the fish markets at Port Elizabeth and East London. Pilchards or sardines are rarely to be had fresh, but are mainly used for canning; Butterfish, perhaps the most tasty of all, is a deep-sea species only occasionally seen on the fish stalls.

There are many kinds of fresh water fish, among them being the mackerel, yellow fish, carp, barbel and trout, but they can seldom be bought.

Cape cooks dealt with all fish in various ways that were all modifications of traditional recipes. Large fish were cut up; we have no recipe for preparing for the table a 14 or 15 lb. fish. Moderate sized specimens might on occasion be brought to table in their entirety, plain steamed or water sootjied, and served with butter sauce. But most recipes direct that the fish should be cut into small square pieces, known as *mootjies*, or filleted; skins and bones were used for making fish stock. Very little water was used for boiling, and the best recipes always prescribe boiling in a coulis, prepared with sliced onions, spice, herbs and a glass of wine or vinegar; sometimes a court bouillon is to be used.

Grilled fish was plainly cooked on the gridiron over the coals; for frying, lard or sheeptail fat was used; and deep frying, in which the food was plunged into boiling oil or fat, was not favoured. Baking was not commonly used, but stewing, braising and slow simmering were popular methods of dealing with dried fish. Marinades of various kinds were employed, and batter was occasionally used when frying.

Fish was usually cooked as fresh as possible, although

52

expert cooks declared that they should not "come fresh **fish** from the water" but should be allowed to lie for some hours before being subjected to heat. Out of season they were regarded as indifferent, some kinds even as unwholesome. The roes and livers of a few kinds were esteemed as delicacies.

One of the best known fish dishes at the Cape is also one of the oldest and is undoubtedly of Eastern origin. It is known as *ingelegde vis*, which is commonly Englished into "curried fish", although it should properly be called a pickled fish curry. It is never eaten hot but always cold, and must be allowed to stand for a week or a fortnight before it is served. It may be packed in jars with a layer of fat on top and will in that way keep for several months.

Ingelegde vis. Choose a fairly firm-fleshed fish, such as geelbek or yellowtail; softer kinds, such as stock or kabeljou, will not keep as long. Clean and cut up* the fish into equal sized pieces about three inches square; fry them in lard without previously dusting them with flour or covering them with batter; strew some salt on them and let them drain while you are making the pickle.

For this you lightly brown sliced onions and a bruised garlic clove, a couple of crushed chillies, a dozen black peppercorns, a tablespoonful of moist brown sugar, and one or two lemon or bay leaves, stirring them constantly till they are well braised. Then add half a cupful of good curry powder, mixed with two cups of good vinegar, and let it simmer for a quarter of an hour. Now add enough vinegar to make the pickle into a fairly thick liquid. Put some of this at the bottom of the dish in which you intend to keep the fish, and put on it a layer of fried fish; cover with more pickle and proceed in the same way till the dish is full.

Mix what remains of the sauce with more curry powder, boil it up with two cups of vinegar and pour this thin sauce over the fish. Put aside in a cool place for several days and serve when required with thin bread and butter.

This recipe, which is the oldest that I have been able to find, is perhaps not definite enough. The onion "rings" should remain whole, although properly cooked, and the dish is really a series of curried fried fish layers embedded in layers of fried onion, and saturated with a sour-sweet, spiced pickle. It is also greatly improved by the addition of a little tamarind juice and is, of course, much more fragrant when it is made with freshly-prepared curry paste.

A variant of this dish is the *penang vis*, prepared as follows:

Make a good fish stock from fish bones, herbs, sliced green ginger, peppercorns and a couple of lemon leaves.

*Note that the fish is not boned. In properly made ingelegde vis the bones are so soft that they can be eaten without harm, thereby much increasing the nourishing qualities of the dish!

fish Strain, then brown in butter or fat a couple of sliced onions, with a tiny morsel of garlic, a teaspoonful of brown sugar, one of salt and a large tablespoonful of curry powder, mixing all with sufficient vinegar or lemon juice to make a paste. Pour on this the fish stock, and let it slowly simmer for a few minutes. Add to it fillets of raw fish; let them boil for ten or fifteen minutes, and serve hot, with boiled rice and potatoes.

Less watery, but hardly less appetising, are the penangs in which no fish stock is used but the fillets are gently braised in the curry sauce. These are really fish curries, and are immensely improved by the addition of coconut milk and chillies. The penangs made with fish stock are variations of bouillabaise, and there are many recipes for them, in some of which saffron is used.

Fish cakes, variously styled *fish balls, fish frikkadels,* and *fish dumplings,* are things quite different from the dry tasteless namesakes that figure on so many bills of fare and are nowadays usually concocted from tinned fish. According to the old recipes they are all made from raw or cooked fish, carefully boned and vigorously pounded in the mortar, always in fellowship with butter or cream, wine, spices and herbs; sometimes too with the addition of blanched almonds and chutney. This paste, sweetly smooth and soft and exquisitely flavoured, was then rolled into tiny balls, patted into neat little cakes, or shaped as small rolls, boiled in fish stock or carefully fried in fat, and served always with the accompaniment of a moderately sharp sauce. Sometimes the fish paste was pounded with bread soaked in milk and the fish cakes were dusted with bread crumbs before being fried. The result was generally a soft, well-cooked, and appetising dish, which could stand on its own merits or suffer the company of some neutral vegetable such as boiled rice. When eaten cold, it went admirably with a simple salad. Similar cakes were made from fish's roe or fish liver, but in these eggs were generally used to bind the ingredients.

Fish with eggs. The ordinary fish omelet was well known, but a more interesting dish was made in accordance with the recipes that are taken from a late eighteenth century manuscript book:

Clean and carefully bone some pieces of raw fish and lightly fry them in fat or butter, with a crushed chilli, a blade of mace, some onion rings, a pinch of ginger, a sprig of thyme, a sprig of rosemary, and salt and pepper to taste. When nicely braised, stir in your eggs, which you have beaten up with a teaspoonful of old wine or brandy. Cook till the eggs are set and serve at once.

Take pieces of dried fish (snoek or herring). Soak in water, bone, and braise with onions, spices and herbs, in plenty of butter. When properly braised, add a spoonful of cream and one of wine or brandy and simmer; stir in beaten eggs, and serve.

In both these dishes the result should be of the con- **fish** sistency of buttered eggs, light, rich and succulent. The colour is always improved by adding a little saffron (which should be steeped in wine for a few minutes before being added). The chilli may be omitted, but it does add to the piquancy of the dish. Crayfish flesh may be substituted for the fish and makes an excellent variant.

Fish bobotie is simply a bobotie in which fish has been substituted for meat and may be called a baked fish pudding. The oldest recipe for it is the following:

Pound raw or cooked fish, after having carefully removed all bones, with a couple of slices of white bread soaked in milk, a blade of mace, a few sprigs of parsley, marjoram and thyme, a pinch of black pepper, a pinch of powdered ginger, a teaspoonful of salt and a tablespoonful of brown sugar. Brown some slices of onion in fat with, if you care to add them, a clove of garlic and a crushed red chilli. Add to it two teaspoonsful of curry powder stirred into a cupful of tamarind water, or vinegar if you have no tamarind in the pantry. Let this sauce simmer for a few minutes, and then stir into it your fish paste. Work it smoothly with a wooden spoon and add coconut water or cream. Cook for ten minutes. Place it into a pie dish, coated inside with butter; put blanched almonds on top, pour over all a couple of eggs beaten up with salt, nutmeg and a few spoonsful of unskimmed milk and bake it in the oven "until a knife blade comes out of it clean." Serve with boiled rice.

For an old *Fish pudding* there are these directions.

What is left over of your boiled elf, you may, if you are frugal (sic), use for a made dish which the good man will like as much as the children. You must take of the flesh three quarters of a pound, and free it from bones, skin and gristle; then you must beat it to a smooth paste, adding salt, pepper, mace and ginger. When it is smooth you must add to it, gradually, so as to mix thoroughly with the paste, half a cup of onion that you have chopped up very fine and previously scalded, and then you must stir the paste into half a gill of cream with which you have beaten up the yolks of six eggs and put it all in your buttered pudding form which you must cover with a cloth and place in a pot of water to boil steadily. It is good to eat, either hot immediately when cooked or, better still, cold with pickles the day after you have made it. Aunt G—— always adds a quarter of a pound of butter to the paste, but that tends to make it too heavy.

Experimentally, I have found that a little butter added improves this dish, which is made still better if the despised whites of the eggs are lightly whipped and incorporated with the paste before it is boiled. A melted butter sauce, soured with a little lemon juice, is the proper thing to serve with it.

The *kedgerees*, of which there are several varieties, **are**

fish fish pilafs — that is to say more or less dry risottos with fish as the principal protein ingredient. The generic recipe for them is the following:

Another way to use what is left over from your boiled fish is to make of it a kitshiri such as they prepare in the Indies. For this you must boil a cupful of rice and set it aside to swell and dry. Your fish you must chop fine, removing from it all bones and mixing it with hard-boiled eggs which you have also chopped up, in the proportion of two eggs to every cupful of fish. Put into a flat pan a few onion rings, a chilli, some pepper, nutmeg and salt, and fry lightly in butter. Then add a large lump of butter and when it is melted stir in the rice, fish and chopped egg, and let it simmer, shaking the pan until everything has been well soaked and blended. You may eat it with chutney as they do in the Indies.

It should be quite dry and not the least greasy. All sorts of experimental modifications may be made of this dish. Some incorporated grated cheese with it; some a little curry powder; and some, to give it more piquancy, chopped anchovies. An interesting kedgeree is made with the claw flesh of the crayfish and hard-boiled penguin egg, but the taste is perhaps a bit too pronounced for most palates. Crab meat makes an excellent kedgeree and so does the flesh of the pearl mussel. Instead of being fried in the way indicated, the mixture may be packed into shells or pannikins and baked in the oven.

Allied to the kedgerees, but more strongly flavoured, are the varieties of *gesmoorde vis*, which is "smothered fish" in literal translation but in practice is usually dried fish, salted and wind dried, braised with onions and potatoes. The typical recipe is for *gesmoorde snoek:*

Put the pieces of fish in fresh water for an hour; throw the water off and boil the pieces in fresh water for 15 minutes. Take them out, remove all bones, and break up into small pieces. Braise sliced onions in a little fat or butter; add a crushed chilli, pepper, salt, a sprinkling of powdered ginger and a teaspoonful of brown sugar and floury, cooked potatoes cut into slices. Put the fish into this and let it slowly simmer, adding butter if it is too dry. Serve with rice.

This dish should be pungent, spicy, and satisfying, and neither too dry nor too moist. Care is necessary to strike the true mean, but is well repaid by the excellent result.

Somewhat similar is a *vis bredie* or fish stew:

Cut up raw or cooked fish into small, neat pieces, from which the bones should be removed. Put them into a saucepan with butter, a cupful of chopped celery, a similar quantity of peeled and diced potatoes, a couple of sliced onions, half a clove of garlic, a crushed chilli, a teaspoonful of brown sugar, a sprinkling of powdered ginger, half a teaspoonful of white pepper, and salt to taste; add a small cupful of fish or meat stock. Put on the

56

fire with the lid on the saucepan, and let simmer, shaking fish carefully to prevent burning. The longer and more slowly it stews, the better will be the result. When the stew is ready, stir in a cupful of boiled rice and a tablespoonful of soya sauce. Let it simmer for another quarter of an hour and serve.

Fish simply prepared is sometimes, especially where the more delicate kinds are concerned, the best way in which to cook it. Elf is one of the best Cape fishes, and the recipe for dealing with it may serve as a model for other sorts:

Clean the fish, and rub it with mint leaves. Lay it in a fish pan and strew over it some shallots, a sprig of rosemary, a blade of mace, some peppercorns and a little salt. Pour over all enough white wine to cover it. Put the lid on and bring to the boil. Let it boil gently for some minutes; remove and drain and serve at once with a sour butter sauce.

The same method may be followed in the case of stockfish (hake) which is now obtainable, thanks to cold storage, practically all the year round, although it is essentially a summer fish (like elf) and practically all kinds of soft-fleshed fish. There are innumerable recipes for boiling such kinds, especially sole. Filleted, they may be steamed, simply or stuffed, garnished with various vegetables and fruits – such as peeled fresh grapes, stewed aubergines, loquats or carrots, fried bananas, pineapple slices, or vegetable chips – and sophisticated with accompaniments of various purees.

A few notes on particular kinds of fish may be added. *Galjoen* is supposed to be at its best in the early summer months. It is a coarse fish, its flesh singularly marbled by the large blood vessels and is usually, in season, excessive-

fish ly fat. It is best grilled or broiled over the coals of a wood fire; second best when stuffed and baked in the oven; excellent when planked and served with pickled walnuts; not so good when boiled or piece-fried.

Haarders or mullets are admirable when grilled and served with a butter sauce; boiled or fried, they are insipid and need the encouragement of a good, savoury sauce. Dried, as *bokkoms*, they are very tasty when, after a preliminary soaking to get rid of the excess salt, they are butter-steamed (not fried) in a covered pan and served with a dusting of fried parsley.

Snoek, in season from April to June, is best served grilled or fried in fat or butter in moderate-sized pieces. The belly portion is reckoned the most savoury and is certainly, when the fish is fat, the most delicate part; other parts are, even when carefully cooked, apt to be stringy and dry. It needs the accompaniment of much melted butter. Boiled, it is coarse and flavourless, but when sun-dried it makes excellent and tasty dishes braised, stewed or marinated.

Panger, now rarely obtainable, is in season in June, and most excellent when fried. *Kabeljou* or cod, reputed to be at its best in March, is best plain-boiled, with a butter sauce. *Roman*, in August, is one of the choicest fishes and should be steamed in wine, like *elf*, which is a mid-summer fish, and served with an appropriate sauce. *Hottentot*, in season in September, is best fried. So, too, are the delicate, now alas very rare, *klipfish*. The *kingklip*, *geelbek* and *katonkel* are all firm-fleshed, none particularly delicate in flavour, and all capable of improvement with appropriate treatment with spices and herbs. All three make excellent pickled curried fish and are much in demand for this.

Sole and *skate* are now usually obtained from cold storage and can be prepared in accordance with the innumerable recipes in all cookery books. There are, so far as I know, no specially local recipes for serving either of them. *Pilchards or sardines* are no longer obtainable fresh; formerly they were, and we then served them crisply fried in fat and found them delicious.

Little need be said about the freshwater fish. Procedures for their tasty preparation are mostly slight variations of the age-old European recipes with the stuffing generally omitted.

Yellowfish, which is found in practically all the rivers in the Cape Province and may attain several pounds in weight, is soft-fleshed, bony, delicately-flavoured, and one of the best freshwater fish for the table. It is generally simply split, salted and peppered, and grilled or broiled over the hot coals, or shallow fried in fat or butter.

An excellent variation is to marinade it as follows:

Mix a half pint of vinegar with the same quantity of red wine, and boil the liquid with a few bay leaves, a couple of shallots, an onion sliced, a dozen allspice, a blade of mace, a dozen black peppercorns, a pinch of powdered or a slice of green ginger, a sprig of rosemary, half a dozen cloves, a

58

crushed chilli, and salt to taste, adding gradually a cup of fish boiling water in which you have mixed a tablespoonful of chutney sauce (blatjang). Put the whole yellowfish, carefully scraped and gutted and rubbed with a morsel of garlic, into the boiling liquid; add a large lump of butter, and allow to boil gently for half an hour; draw the pot aside and allow the fish to get cold in the marinade. Serve with any salad sauce.

Any soft-fleshed sea fish may be prepared in a similar way; the marinade may be used several times, provided fresh vinegar and wine are added.

From yellowfish a good *fish sambal* or cold relish can be made:

Pound the cooked fish, from which the bone has been removed, with some raw onion, a tiny scrap of garlic, a pinch of ginger powder, and as much green or red chillies as suits your taste; moisten with lemon juice and incorporate into the paste enough coconut milk to make it moderately soft. Salt to taste and serve on thin bread and butter with some grated carrot over.

Instead of the carrot, crayfish coral may be used, which adds immeasurably to the piquancy of the paste. All sambals must be chilled, and ought not to be over-salted.

Besides fish many other foodstuffs come out of the sea, and of these many are used in Cape cookery. Indeed, it is with this variety of sea-food that the Cape cook, following the old recipes, sometimes creates dishes that have the merit of being original — not merely because some of the ingredients are essentially local, but also because they have been benignly blended to produce some marvellously exhilarating combinations. Various crustaceans, shell-fish and sea weeds are used, with cuttle fish. Something has already been said about the way in which these may be made use of in preparing soups; it remains to detail other methods of preparing them for the table.

Crayfish, now often and quite mistakenly referred to as crawfish, are delectable eating, specially when you can procure them live. Ordinarily crayfish are exposed for sale when they have already been boiled, and that indeed is nowadays the only way in which the average cook can get hold of them. Boiled crayfish claws are also sold by the pound. The fastidious cook will make a point of securing a live crayfish, and preparing it for all dishes that are to be made from it by first boiling it lightly in a thin, well-spiced and herbed stock. This gives it a mellowness and preserves its soft, delicate taste and fine flavour, both of which are irretrievably lost by quick boiling in salt water. From the flesh of crayfish cooked in such a *coulis* many dishes may be prepared in accordance with the old recipes. Here are a few:

Crayfish salad. Take the flesh from the large and small claws and break it into neat pieces; add to it some of the fish flesh from the tail, diced, and all the soft white and green meat from the inside of the carapace. Mix all this well with salt, pepper, powdered ginger, some finely chopped onion, half a dozen green nasturtium seeds, a little fresh thyme and a few crushed coriander seeds. Beat up three yolks of eggs in a cupful of vinegar with a teaspoonful of lemon juice, salt and pepper to taste, so as to make a smooth cream, and mix with it a few tablespoonsful of pounded blanched almonds. Pour over the fish and let it stand in a cool place for half an hour. Mix thoroughly and serve on lettuce leaves, garnished with slices of hard-boiled eggs and fresh cucumber, and with grated coral all over.

This salad is altogether more piquant and tasty than that usually provided which is simply boiled and served with a mayonnaise or oil and vinegar dressing. Some old cooks made it with the sauce so liberally added that it was almost a gruel, to be eaten with a spoon, but the more conservative way is to have the meat well coated with the sauce. There is a school that prescribes powdered red chilli with it, but I do not subscribe to it, for too much sharpness deprives the flesh of that delicate flavour that the salad should have. When crayfish flesh, already cooked, is reheated in some way, the addition of chillies is sometimes a vast improvement.

Baked crayfish. The meat is pounded with whatever spices, herbs and nuts your fancy may fix on (one of the oldest recipes mentions among the herbs, lavender, among the spices, cardamons, and among the nuts pistachio), butter and soaked bread. It is salted to taste, mixed with cream and put back into the shell, which is then adorned with a few lumps of butter and put into the oven to bake.

There are many variations of this. The pounded flesh is mixed with a white sauce; with grated cheese; with (in recipes that are comparatively modern) tomatoes, avocado pear, mashed potatoes or aubergines; brandy is added, or chopped anchovies – your own imagination will enable you to experiment to your heart's content. You will find that, unless you absolutely drown the crayfish in one particular spice, its flesh blends admirably with nearly everything you can think of; no matter how unskilful your technique is, you can never quite ruin this dish.

Crayfish souffle, on the contrary, demands the most scrupulous care in preparing and cooking. It is made by stirring into a good souffle mixture a white sauce thickened with yolk of egg, the carapace flesh pounded with nutmeg, salt, pepper and a little grated lemon peel, adding a teaspoonful of brandy and whipping in the beaten egg white. After this it is baked in a quick oven and served at once. It should be feathery light, but with enough stamina to make it succulent and tasty.

Crayfish curry is simply the tail flesh diced, stewed in white wine and then braised in butter with curry powder, which should have a good pinch of powdered red chilli **fish** added to it. It should be served with boiled rice, lightly-fried eggs and fried bananas.

Crayfish with pineapple was never a common dish, as the fruit was by no means easy to obtain in the old days. The pineapple was peeled and cored, thinly sliced, and a layer of it was placed in an earthenware dish, powdered with salt, ginger, red pepper and a little rice flour. On this a layer of the fish was placed, after having been lightly braised with some onion rings. Over this came a layer of

apple slices, followed by another layer of fish, covered finally by a top layer of pineapple slices. A cup of wine was poured over and the dish was baked in the oven.

The combination of sweet, spicy pungency and the characteristic crayfish taste is interesting and attractive.

There are similar recipes for ordinary fish, with or without the addition of mussels or oysters.

Crabs are seldom obtainable in sizes that allow them to be treated like crayfish, but when they are available the same recipes will serve for them.

Mussels, of which there are two chief kinds, the large oval white-shelled and the elongated dark blue sort, were generally boiled with a little white wine (after having been washed in fresh water) strained and served in their shells. Sometimes spices and herbs were added to the wine, but usually the mussels were eaten with an appropriate sauce, made by adding vinegar or lemon juice to melted butter beaten up with an egg yolk. Sometimes they were stewed in white wine, braised with leeks or onions, curried or fried in batter. More elaborate dishes were made by mincing them, cooked, mixing with cream, spices and pot herbs, and steaming the mince as a pudding or baking it in the oven.

Limpets, essentially the poor man's dish, needed a little more elaborate treatment:

Take them from their shells, wash them thoroughly in water, remove their fringes and beat them with a wooden mallet or flat stone; after which wash them again, and then dry them in a cloth. In a flat iron stewpot put a large lump of fat and melt; then slice into it a couple of onions, and let them brown; now add the limpets, with a crushed chilli, a dozen peppercorns, a blade of mace, and a handful of small shallots. Put on the lid and let the contents slowly simmer, shaking the pot frequently. After stewing for half an hour,

61

fish add a cupful of wine, a pinch of salt and a teaspoonful of brown sugar; mix all together, and let it simmer till the stew is well combined and the limpets are tender. Serve after thickening the gravy with a little tapioca.

This limpet stew is a most satisfying dish and was a great favourite when limpets were easily procurable. Now one seldom sees it, and even more rarely does one get it well prepared. The secret of success with it (and it is a dish that easily can be ruined) is prolonged, steady, but slow and mild simmering.

The best of all sea-food dishes at the Cape is undoubtedly that made from the flesh of the perlemoen or pearl mussel (*haliotis sp*) which is found below high-water mark on most of the rock ledges along the eastern coast. It varies in size from a couple to 12 inches in diameter, and is a univalve that attaches itself strongly to the rock. It must be first removed from its shell, for which a sharp, strong knife is required, and must then be trimmed of its "beard" or fringe, and cleaned vigorously with a scrubbing brush. We now have a cartilaginously hard substance, ugly looking and unattractive, that must be beaten with a mallet until its rigidity has changed to a texture not unlike that of a raw steak. This is now carefully dried in a clean cloth, and is ready for use.

The mussel, it is pertinent to remark, must be quite fresh; the least taint about it ruins its flavour and makes it tough. However, care taken in this preliminary preparation will be well repaid by the excellence of the cooked result.

Stewed pearl mussel (gestoofde klipkous, perlemoen). Cut the mussels up into equal-sized pieces about two inches square. Take care that no water remains on them. Put them in the pot with a large lump of fat or butter, a blade of mace, a couple of cloves, and a little white pepper, but no salt. Put on the lid and place the pot on the fire, where let the contents simmer, shaking occasionally. The mussel flesh is done when a fork easily sinks in and usually ten minutes simmering will cook them; more may make them stringy. Now add salt, a wineglassful of brandy and a cupful of cream, and let the pieces stew in that for a few minutes. Take them out and put them in the serving dish; thicken the gravy with a little rice flour and serve immediately, grating nutmeg over it.

This superb dish will be spoiled if — as some printed modern recipes direct — any water is used in the process of cooking. Likewise if salt is added before the cooking has made the flesh tender; hence the directive to add the salt, cream and brandy at a later stage. The flesh should be as soft as marrow and yet firm, creamy white, with a peculiar, wholly pleasant, seaweed-like aroma, and a delicate, original taste about which the epicure may rave.

This virgin delicacy should not be marred by overspicing; the mace and the cloves, and later on the zest of the brandy, are all that it needs for its enhancement.

62

However, there are many who think differently, as the **fish** variety of recipes for sophisticating klipkous shows. Some would add to it all kinds of spices – including chillies, which do not blend at all with it, and Worcester sauce, which quite spoils its flavour – and festoon it with potato chips, fried aubergine, aye, and even cauliflower saturated in white sauce. One recipe simmers it with onion. Another mixes it with tomatoes, after boiling it in bouillon – obviously a comparatively modern recipe, echoes from some American cook-book. A third would have you believe that it is improved with a mornay or cheese sauce ; a fourth makes curry of it. Perhaps the only recipe that a conscientious cook can recommend, and that on account of its originality and because it does bring into juxta-position on one's tongue two agreeable tastes at the same time, is that which states that you may, when you have removed the cooked pieces, thicken the gravy, not with tapioca, but with a mixture of white bread crumb and grated ripe, raw quince. Boil this up and pour it over the klipkous before serving.

But this mussel is altogether too delicate and too noble to be cooked in any other style than that described in the first recipe. It is of all South African dishes indubitably the finest when prepared in this way. If any portion of the dish is left over (something that, in my experience, has never happened) you may mince it and make fish cakes of it, or a fine bisque or, best of all, metamorphose it into a klipkous kedgeree that is really a revelation of what such things can be.

Far more strongly-flavoured than perlemoen, and thus not to everyone's liking, are *cuttlefish* and *octopus*, both in great demand by Malay cooks who are connoisseurs and know the good things that come out of the sea. Alive both cephalopods are ugly, unappetising looking objects ; properly cooked they are, for those who like a full-flavoured dish with a dash of the bizarre in it, highly succulent, surprisingly eatable, and wonderfully rich foods. The octopus is known as *fiskat* or fishcat, and the smaller cuttlefish as *tjokka*. The former is regularly used by fishermen for bait, and moderate-sized specimens are not difficult to obtain.

The tentacles are skinned, beaten with a wooden mallet, and cut into medium-sized pieces as a preliminary to any method by which they may be cooked. The tjokka, sometimes still to be found exposed for sale at the fish market, is skinned, the dark-coloured fluid in its "bag" is retained, and its flesh, too, is softened by beating before it is cut up.

The older recipes for both state that the flesh must be cooked in fat or butter, with the addition of a host of spices, herbs and nuts, a glass of brandy and, in the case of the tjokka, the coloured fluid from the head of the beast into which a little rice flour has been stirred. Then it must be allowed to simmer gently for several hours, being frequently shaken to prevent burning. Before serving, a couple of egg yolks, beaten up with a tablespoonful of lemon juice, must be quickly stirred into the gravy and the

fish dish sent to table at once, to be eaten with boiled rice.

More modern recipes favour a treatment in which the flesh is simmered with the flavourings, with tomatoes, and gets a final addition of blanched almonds, pistachios and seeded raisins. It can be braised also in a curry sauce, or stewed with cheese and potatoes.

The main characteristic of a dish made from it must be its full, rich, over-spiced and extraordinarily fragrant quality. For that reason you must not be sparing with the chillies, nor with the herbs; practically every garden herb blends with it, and the greater the variety of flavours the better is the result. Here, too, the flesh must not be water-boiled, else it will get tough and stringy; it should be gently simmered in fat or butter, and only when it is duly soft must the other fluid concomitants of the stew be added.

Oysters and *clams*, both of which are easily procurable as they are to be found in both the Indian Ocean and the Atlantic, were not greatly esteemed. The recipes for their preparation are not older than the early part of the nineteenth century and are all obviously copied from printed cookery books. Some old recipes, however, mention them as additions to meat or fish dishes; for instance, one old recipe for fish bobotie says that "a few oysters will improve this dish".

Eels, too, both the conger and the freshwater variety, although formerly common enough on the market, do not seem to have exercised the special ingenuity of Cape cooks. There are old recipes for their cooking, but I have not been able to find any that differ in essentials from those printed in European books before 1750. Later on, obviously under the Oriental influence, an "eel stew" was directed to be made with the addition of "chillies, garden sage, green ginger, verbena and allspice and peppercorns". There is also a recipe for an eel sambal which is merely a variant of that for the fish sambal already mentioned.

I have once eaten, at the old White House Hotel in Strand Street, where the coloured cook — my most proficient instructress in the art of making pancakes — used fish and eel flesh for the dish, a delectable *eel pancake*, made as follows:

Pound the flesh of grilled eel in a mortar, separating the bones; add to it melted butter, cream, grated nutmeg, a drop of anchovy sauce, pepper and salt, and a few drops of rum. Make paper-thin pancakes from a batter of eggs, sifted flour and salt; cover them with the paste and roll them up. Place in a dish, grate over a little nutmeg, place in the oven to keep warm, and serve with chutney.

Any fish or meat paste can be used; the pancakes should be light, very thin, and succulent, and the warmth of the oven must be only enough to heat the paste without making its covering tough.

Sea-weed dishes may, perhaps, more appropriately be dealt with in the chapter on vegetables. It may be said

that old Cape cooks liked on occasion to put a handful of **fish**
sea weed in the court bouillon in which they cooked fish,
and sometimes permitted a few shreds to share in the
flavouring of fish stews. The variety favoured for making
jellies was also employed in soup making and in fact replaced, round about 1825, the expensive birds nests from
Java that were deemed indispensable for a jellied consommé.

Chapter VI

MEAT AND
MEAT DISHES

MEAT has always been man's chief food. For all that faddists may say, meat and wine and oil and wheat make a diet that can sustain the human body in perfect health, and for this reason meat has always ranked first among the available foodstuffs in both civilised and barbarian communities. It is therefore reasonable to expect that more care and attention have been bestowed on its culinary improvement than on other foodstuffs, and that the variations in recipes for its preparation for consumption exceed in number those for any other class of food.

At the Cape the earliest settlers found an abundance of meat, chiefly beef, that was, and remains still, of inferior quality, lacking that close intermixture of fat with muscle fibre that distinguishes stall-fed beef. The mutton, however, was beautifully tender, deliciously fat, and usually, on account of the aromatic veld bush on which the sheep fed, exceedingly well flavoured. Pork and poultry meat were introduced, but there were many different kinds of wild animals that yielded good meat, and from the earliest times these were killed and eaten. In general, the recipes for meat dishes were copied from instructions in printed

66

books, but there were many local adaptations and im- **meat**
provements, both in methods of cooking and in the use
of accessories to improve the flavour and succulence of
the dishes.

Beef was nearly always pot-roasted, boiled, pickled or
dried to form *biltong* or *tassal*. Minced or pounded it was
used for sausages and frikkadels. The best cooks larded
it with fat pork and it was rarely grilled or fried, though on
occasion one comes across a recipe for a "fried steak"
or "beef chops". Only when no other meat was obtainable was it used for stews or bredies, for which mutton
was much preferred. With pork, it was the meat most
often salted or pickled for long sea voyages, and in its
dried form it was the main item in the commissariat of
those who undertook inland trips, for there are few more
satisfying and nutritious snacks than a thick slice of bread
and butter overlaid with snippets of home-made biltong.

Many kinds of dishes were prepared from the internal
organs of the ox — the brains, liver, heart, kidneys, sweetbreads, tongue and tripe being used — while stock was
made from the bones, and a strong, jellied consommé
from the gelatinous parts. Farcing was rarely used for beef,
but was extensively employed with other meats, and a
few words may here be interpolated about farces that
play an important part in meat cookery.

Properly speaking a farce is a filling or stuffing round
which the meat is wrapped so that its flavouring can per-
meate the meat from within outwards. Larding is, after all,
merely a variant of farcing in this sense, although its pri-
mary intention is not to flavour but to fatten the meat.
Finicky cooks divide farces into two main kinds, but in
practice no such demarcation line need be drawn. The
principal farces used in Cape cookery are the following.

Vetvulsel (fatty stuffing) used for any meat dish. Mince
six ounces of kidney suet with bread crumbs, chopped
shallots, parsley, thyme, nutmeg, salt and pepper, and mix
with two tablespoonsful unskimmed milk and the yolks of
two eggs, till the mixture is smooth and stiff. To this can
be added the minced cooked liver of a hare, a muscovy
duck, goose or calf, when the mixture is known as a liver
stuffing.

Onion farce (uie vulsel). Braise four minced onions
with a handful of minced sage leaves and six ounces of
bread crumbs in a little butter or fat; season with salt and
pepper. This is used for poultry and pork dishes.

Oyster farce (oester vulsel). Chop a dozen fresh oysters
or clams, and mix with four ounces breadcrumbs, an
ounce and a half of salted butter, a pinch of grated nutmeg,
some finely-chopped marjoram and parsley leaves, a
small fragment of chilli, the juice of one large lemon, and
the yolk of an egg; add some of the native liquid of the
oysters; form the mixture into small patties or balls (this
needs some skill; most cooks therefore make it easier, but
no better, by adding more breadcrumb and butter) and use

meat immediately for stuffing fish or poultry.

Almond farce (amandel vulsel). Beat three egg yolks with a cupful of cream and a pinch of grated nutmeg. Pound three ounces of blanched almonds in a mortar with a little of the white of egg, and stir into the beaten egg yolk, with six ounces of fine bread crumbs and two ounces fresh butter diced. Beat quickly and add the rest of the whites, whipped to a stiff froth, and continue beating till it is smooth and moderately stiff. Use as a stuffing for poultry.

Baked farce (gebakte vulsel). Mix suet, finely chopped, with breadcrumbs, grated lemon rind, pepper, salt and nutmeg, and incorporate in it enough yolk of egg to make into a stiff paste. Shape into small balls, roll in sifted flour and bake lightly in the oven. Use for stuffing poultry. By mixing minced ham with this paste we get *ham farce*, which need not be baked previously.

Brain farce (harsingvulsel). Lightly cook sheep's or calf's brains in butter or white wine, and pound in a mortar with pepper, salt, parsley, a little onion juice and a few drops of rum. Make into a stiff paste with egg yolk and white bread soaked in milk from which all the milk has been squeezed out; shape into small balls, roll in sifted flour and bake lightly. Stuff poultry with this.

Curry stuffing (kerrievulsel), *egg stuffing* (eiervulsel), *crayfish stuffing* (kreefvulsel), *avocado-pear stuffing* (avocadopeervulsel) and *tomato stuffing* (tamatievulsel) are all made in the same way, using respectively curry powder, pounded hard-boiled egg yolks, the pounded flesh of crayfish, mashed raw avocado pear, and tomato puree, instead of brain paste.

Stuffing for a sucking pig (speenvarkvulsel). Mince, but do not pound, sliced onion, sage leaves, thyme, marjoram, green ginger, mace and plenty of green chillies. Mix with bread crumbs and salt, and make into a stiff paste with egg yolk and a little brandy. Stuff the pig tightly with this mixture, and sew up well.

I have learned by experiment that this farce may be improved by the addition of a couple of pittosporum leaves.

Dried fruit stuffing (droëvrugtevulsel.) Soak dried apricots, prunes and peaches, equal quantities of each, in wine or water; remove stones from prunes and place the soaked fruit in a saucepan with some tamarind, sugar, tangerine peel, ginger, a few cloves and a feather of cinnamon; cover with wine, and boil gently. Remove from the liquid and place in a dry saucepan, with a large lump of butter. Let the butter melt and shake the pot so that the fruit becomes well coated with the butter. Use as a filling for poultry or sucking-pig. Handle carefully so that the fruit remains whole.

Fresh fruit is used in the same way to make a farce. **meat**
Stewed fruit is often served, whole or as a puree, with
roasted meat. A well-known, though not often used,
recipe is that for baking a lamb with a fruit stuffing. The
lamb is coated inside with butter or fat, and then filled
with pomegranate seeds, pistachio nuts, preserved dates,
citron and a few chopped rose apples mixed with a little
dried ginger and tangerine peel. It is then slowly roasted
or baked, being frequently basted with a mixture of wine
and vinegar. The result is excellent. Many modifications
of this essentially Persian recipe exist.

Green mielie stuffing (groen-mielievulsel). **This is
simply fresh, young mielies, cut off the cob, mixed with
spices and herbs, some cream and the yolk of eggs, and
stiffened with breadcrumbs. Some cooks add a few drops
of rum.**

There is, of course, no end to the variations in the compo-
sition of farces. The main consideration is that the flavour
of whatever combination is used should not be so strong
and definite as to impair the flavour of the meat; therefore
garlic and chillies are infrequently mentioned among the
ingredients, preference being given to spices and herbs
that blend more easily.

There are old-fashioned recipes that tell of a stuffing
within a stuffing; one of the most curious of these is the
recipe that directs that a large sucking pig should be
coated inside with its proper farce, and then be filled with
partridges stuffed with a liver paste. My own experience
is that the partridges are most excellent, but that the pig
differs in no manner from one that has been roasted in a
less elaborate manner.

All kinds of vegetables are used for farcing, sometimes
whole but more often in the shape of a fairly thick puree,
adequately seasoned, and properly used these fillings
greatly improve the taste of wild birds and some domestic
fowl. But be careful with celery; if you want your meat
to have a distinctive but not too strong taste of celery,
feed the fowl on the chopped leaves some weeks before
it is killed. Nuts, too, are often useful as a paste for
farcing, as their sweetish taste is generally agreeable; an
exception is ground-nuts whose flavour, when heated, is
apt to be too strong.

No useful purpose would be served, and much room
would be taken up, by describing the various ways in
which different kinds of meat can be cooked. Let me
therefore confine my remarks to a few recipes which may
be considered traditional in South Africa, although none
of them can be claimed to be strictly speaking original,
as each has its counterpart in the cookery of other lands.

Mutton. Cape mutton is generally excellent. The best
comes from the Karoo farms or from the grasslands of
Natal or the Free State, but a particularly fine quality
stems from the Sandveld of the South Western districts of
the Cape Province where the sheep browse on halophytic
shrubs. In the butchers' shops one obtains cold storage

meat mutton or mutton from sheep that have been over-driven; this sort of mutton does not do justice to the excellence that characterises the flesh of farm-fed sheep. Lamb is commonly slaughtered too old, and is not of the same quality, though it can be very good indeed. Well fed farm sheep are always fat, and mutton from them sometimes needs considerable trimming, and certainly never needs larding. It is always succulent, delicately flavoured, and tender.

Mutton chops made from Karoo sheep are a joy. They are trimmed, lightly beaten, dusted with fine breadcrumb, and grilled on the gridiron. In the open air they can be wrapped in vine or lettuce leaves and grilled over the fire made with the rhenoster bush (*elytropappus rhinocerotis*) the smoke of which imparts to the meat a distinct and attractive flavour. They are also fried in a thin batter, or braised with onions and spices and herbs, dashed with a little wine, dusted with pepper and served with boiled rice.

Boiled mutton according to the old recipes was something different from the tasteless, stringy meat, served with caper sauce, that is commonly dished up in restaurants:

Trim a leg of mutton; wash it and wrap in a wet cloth. In a large saucepan, which you have filled with water and white wine, half and half, slice a handful of carrots, an onion, two shallots, a dozen cloves, a crushed chilli, half a dozen black peppercorns and a tablespoonful of coarse salt. Let it come to the boil and when it properly bubbles, unwrap your mutton and plunge it into the pot; let it boil quickly for ten minutes; then draw the pot aside and allow it to boil gently till the meat is cooked down to the bone. Take out the meat and put it in a dish in the oven, leaving the oven door open. Braise some young carrots in butter, whole, and arrange them round the meat. Make a white sauce with flour, the water in which the mutton has been boiled and the yolk of an egg; salt and pepper it, and thin it with white wine and lemon juice. Pour over the mutton and serve.

Goat's meat was, and still is, extensively eaten. While it is commonly supposed to be tougher, stringier, and leaner than mutton, it need not therefore be despised, for it can be obtained, on occasion, of a quality that after making allowance for the coarser taste, compares very favourably with ordinary butcher's mutton. Goat's meat of such a quality makes excellent grilled chops; indeed in all the recipes for mutton, goat's meat can be substituted for the mutton, although the result will not be quite the same as when good mutton is used. Where salt mutton is prescribed, as for example, in the recipe for *sout ribbetjie*, goat's flesh serves equally well.

It is usually far stronger in flavour, and in some cases, where the animals have fed on highly aromatic shrubs, its taste may be repugnant and must be overcome by using strong spices. In that case it is best served as a curry or

70

as a "black sour stew". A goat's head and trotters make **meat**
excellent brawn, and its tripe is not to be distinguished
from that of the sheep.

Soesaties (curried kabobs). There are many recipes for
this Indian dish. The generic one is the following:

Take two pounds of fillet of pork, a quarter of a pound
of pork fat from which you have removed the rind, and two
pounds of loin of mutton, from which you have removed all
bone, gristle and membrane. Cut the meat into neat two-
inch square pieces. Mix them and powder them with
ginger, white pepper and salt. Put a layer of them at the
bottom of an earthenware jar and cover it with a thin
layer of very lightly braised onion; strew coriander seeds
and some minced chilli over; add similar layers till the jar
is nearly full, placing a few dried apricots, seeded raisins,
a couple of bay leaves and some slices of green ginger in
the middle layers. Now braise some sliced onions in a deep
saucepan, with four tablespoonfuls of good curry powder,
a large tablespoonful of moist brown sugar, adding butter
or fat till you have a rich curry sauce. Pour on it a bottle of
good vinegar mixed with half a bottle of wine, and let it
boil up. As soon as it comes to the boil, pour the liquid
over the meat.

Let it stand in a cool place for three or four days, shaking
well occasionally, so as to let the marinade percolate
through. For cooking, string the bits of meat on bamboo
skewers, putting a piece of mutton alternately with a
piece of pork and a piece of the pork fat in the middle and
at the end of each skewer. Grill on the gridiron. Boil up the
pickle, till it is a thick sauce. Pour over the cooked skewered
meat and serve with rice, fried bananas and fried eggs.

Variations: add a cupful of milk to the marinade when
it has stood for 24 hours; instead of wine and vinegar,
use half a pound of tamarind steeped in white wine; use
raw, instead of lightly braised onions between the layers;
omit the raisins and apricots and substitute a handful of
blanched almonds. A few blanched almonds in the sauce,
and the use of tamarind instead of vinegar certainly
greatly adds to the piquancy of the dish, while the addition of milk imparts to it a blandness that contrasts well
with the extreme pungency that the chillies give to it.

Soesaties, when properly made, should be tender and
tasty, yet with a crispness that rivals a grilled chop, and
bitingly spicy yet with a suavity that rivals the best made
curry. At a pinch they may be made wholly of mutton, but
in that case pork fat must be used more prodigally. They
should be grilled to a turn and no more, and the curry
sauce should be piping hot. If they are properly spiced,
the fried bananas and the lightly fried eggs that should
accompany them are very welcome to moderate the
aromatic fierceness of the sauce.

A variant of them is *kabobs*, which are simply bits of
meat, previously marinaded in spiced wine and vinegar,
skewered on bits of bamboo alternatively with sections of
tomatoes and onions, fried in a shallow saucepan with

meat mutton fat, and served with a chutney sauce, no curry being used. With them, as well as with soesaties, it is customary to serve fresh *sambals* and chutney.

A soesatie course is in reality a mild imitation of the familiar *rystafel* of Java, in which a number of dishes, always including at least two meat, one fish, and a curry dish and several vegetables, fried potatoes, fried bananas, fried eggs, fried aubergines and crumbled dried fish, are served on a plateful of rice and mixed with a strong curry soup or sauce, to be eaten with a spoon.

Another modification is *penangvleis* which is made in the same way as penang fish already mentioned.

There are various *curries* (kerrievleis) made from mutton, pork, or poultry. In all of them the meat, braised with some onions and a tinge of garlic, with the addition of various fragrant herbs, is finally simmered in a rich curry sauce. If a wet curry is wanted, coconut milk is added and stirred into the brew, which is allowed to continue simmering till it has to be served. If a dry curry is preferred, the cooking is done in an open saucepan, to allow much of the liquid to evaporate, and it must then be frequently shaken to prevent burning, the slightest sign of which spoils any curry.

A mild curry is made without chillies or much pepper and the addition of more sugar and plenty of coconut milk; a hot curry is surcharged with chillies, ginger and pepper, and has much tamarind in it; a black curry which is superlatively pungent is made by adding burnt sugar to the tamarind juice and using much black pepper in powder. Expert cooks always preferred to make their curry powder fresh, by pounding green ginger, cardamons, chillies, peppercorns, cloves, mace, fennel, cumin and aniseed, coriander, garlic and turmeric into a paste, which is mixed with tamarind juice before it is stirred into the braise. Such a curry paste makes a much more delicious curry than most of the commercial curry powders, and even now can be made at home quite easily.

While pork and mutton were preferred for making curries, poultry flesh was sometimes used. A good recipe for a *chicken curry* runs as follows:

Let me implore you not to choose any old rooster for your curry; select a youngster, or two or three of them if you have many guests. Singe it well, and cut it up nicely, but take pains not to crush the bones, for a splinter (as I have myself observed) may cause great discomfort and annoyance to the eater. Lay the pieces on a pan and brown them in butter. Braise your onions, which you must cut up into thin slices, in butter or fat, with a couple of sour apples sliced, a spoonful of brown sugar, and a teaspoonful of salt. Mix a couple of spoonfuls of curry powder with some tamarind water or vinegar and add to the onions; let it simmer and then add the pieces of chicken. Cover the pot, and let all simmer quietly for a couple of hours, shaking the pot frequently; add a few tablespoonsful of coconut milk and let the curry brew gently on the side of the stove until you serve it up with boiled rice and chutney.

72

Boerwors (farm sausage) is now a thing of the past, **meat** although it often appears on the table — a travesty of what it should be and a disgrace to the modern cook. Formerly it was made principally of pork, with a small amount of mutton and beef added. The meat was chosen with care, all gristle being rejected, and was always pounded in the mortar as there were no mincing machines in the olden days, but it is really better to mince it finely by passing it through the machine two or three times. The mince was

mixed with finely-diced pork fat, powdered ginger, mace, cloves, nutmeg, fennel, coriander, thyme, rosemary and mint, pepper and salt, and a mixture of equal parts of wine and vinegar was worked into it. Then it was stuffed into long skins, suspended for a few days in a cool place and fried in a pan or, better still, grilled over the coals. No fat was used; the diced pork gave sufficient fatty substance to the sausage and prevented it from burning.

Such boerwors was a treat to eat when fried, and it was almost as good when it was dried and eaten raw, in slices spread on buttered brown farm bread fresh from the oven. The substitute that we get for it nowadays is a tasteless, anaemic thing, compounded chiefly of gristle and stale bread, generally without any blending of spices within it, and always without any savouriness.

Meat frikkadels, meat cakes, patties or mince, were compounded of minced meat, spices, herbs, cream and wine or vinegar, made into various shapes, and generally shallow-fried in fat, alone or in company with sliced onions. Such meat pastes were sometimes boiled or baked in shallow dishes, with various ingredients added to them — indeed the recipes for them abound, for they were favourite ways of dealing with left-overs from the joint or boiled meat.

An almost indigenous minced meat dish is *bobotie*, which was, however, known in Europe in the middle ages when the Crusaders brought turmeric from the East. The oldest recipe I have is one of the seventeenth century:

To make a Bobootie it is necessary to have clean hands,

73

meat for you must knead the meat as you do a dough. Take, then, of tender mutton and the backstring (fillet) of pork, of each a pound in weight, and that without fat or hard part; pound it vigorously in your mortar, with a handful of blanched almonds, 12 pepper corns, a slice of green ginger, a chilli, a leaf of the herb marjoram, some coriander seeds, a very small piece of fresh garlic, or if you have none of it, half a leaf of an onion, and the grated rind of a lemon, and work into it half a cupful of wine in which you have soaked an ounce of tamarind. Let it stand overnight. Then beat into it half a cupful of cream and two tablespoonsful of good butter, not too much salt, and knead it well. Shape it into a round loaf and put it into an earthenware pie-dish that you have well smeared inside with butter and sprinkled with a few cumin seeds.

Put it in the oven and when it gets hot and expands, but not before, pour over it two cups of milk in which you have beaten up the yolks of three eggs and a tablespoonful of curry powder such as you may get at the Malay store. Let it bake till it is well set, and then put upon it a few blanched almonds and a grating of nutmeg. Before you send it to table you may, if you are not pleased with its top colour, pass a hot salamander over it.

Another recipe says that the curry powder should be mixed with the mince, and the custard added before the baking; another advises that a couple of bay leaves should be added. I cannot honestly affirm that either modification improves the dish, and have found lemon or pittosporum leaves to blend better with the mixture, although it can do very well without them. A Bobotie should be marrow-soft, melting on the tongue, and is best eaten with white, not yellow, rice, with a moderately-sharp chutney as accompaniment.

Smoorvleis or stewed (smothered) meat. Cut the meat — which should preferably be mutton or veal or pork — into small, equal sized pieces, rejecting all gristly bits, and dry and coat them with sifted flour. Put into a pot with onion slices, salt and pepper, a little brown suger, a bruised chilli, a few cloves, a blade of mace and some powdered ginger; add a large lump of sheep tail fat. Cover the pot and place on the fire and as soon as the fat has melted, add a cupful of wine, or stock. Put the lid on and allow the meat to simmer gently for several hours, shaking frequently; finally add a glass of sherry, and thicken the gravy with a little brown roux.

A *white smoorvleis*, which is really a blanquette, is made in the same way, but the braising is allowed to go on just long enough to slightly brown the meat, when a thin white sauce is added and the cooking is continued till the stew is ready. Here the secret is to cook gently, but continuously, and there is little chance of overdoing it if the heat is steady. Both dishes are excellent and not too strongly spiced, but the chillies may be left out if desired.

Sout ribbetjie (salted rib of mutton). Choose the whole **meat** rib of a lamb or part of that of a full-grown sheep. Trim it, and rub it well with a mixture of one part salt and one part of salpetre, coriander seed, pepper and ginger mixed. Lay it on a layer of this mixture in a cool place, and continue rubbing in the salt the next day. Allow it to hang in a draught, and rub in more of the mixture each day for several days, adding to the salt mixture on the second day an equal part of moist brown sugar. In a week's time it will be ready for cooking. You can then grill it whole on the gridiron or, if you prefer it, you can remove the rib bones, cut the meat into pieces and after parboiling it in wine, shallow fry it in a pan or again roast it. The meat should have a fine pink colour, and should be salty and spicy, without being too much so. It is preferably served with "wet rice", which is rice that has been boiled to a mushy softness.

Swart suur (black sour braised meat). Take ribs of mutton, cut them into convenient pieces, without removing the bone; two pounds of the meat is convenient. Braise them in a pot with some onions and a little fat; add a cup of wine, and let simmer; skim off the fat; stir in salt and pepper, a cupful of tamarind water, a teaspoonful of grated nutmeg and one of powdered cloves and a bruised chilli. Simmer for an hour, add a cupful of red wine, and let it boil; then add some small dumplings, made of sifted flour, whipped white of egg and a little melted butter. As soon as the dumplings are cooked serve with boiled rice and potatoes.

Some cooks add blood to this braise, and others prefer to thicken it with brown roux.

An old-fashioned, extremely savoury, *toad-in-the-hole* (padda in die gat) is made as follows:

Make a batter with two cups of sifted flour, a teaspoonful of salt, a little bicarbonate of soda, half a cupful of soft chicken fat, and two cupfuls of buttermilk. Cut up a couple of pounds of tender mutton without any bones into small pieces, each the size of a half crown and about an inch thick; flour them and put them in a pie dish, preferably a very deep one, and sprinkle over them salt, pepper, grated nutmeg, a blade of mace rubbed fine, and a few coriander seeds. Add a glass of wine and another of orange and lemon juice mixed. Pour the batter over, and bake in the oven for a couple of hours.

The bredies. These are combinations of meat with vegetables so intimately stewed that the flesh is thoroughly impregnated with the vegetable flavour while the vegetables have benefited from the meat juices. Almost any vegetable, and several fruits, can be used for bredies, but the only meat that is really suitable is a mutton rib cut up into appropriate sizes, care being taken that no slivers of bone are allowed to enter the stew. The essential steps are that the meat is first braised in butter or fat,

meat with spices, herbs and onions. The vegetables, always raw (except in a very few cases where parboiling is necessary to get rid of some constituent) and generally sliced or minced, are then added, with salt and a cup of water, wine or stock, and the whole is allowed to simmer gently for several hours, the pot being kept closed but frequently shaken and great care being taken that the contents do not burn. Bredies, whether made with chillies or not, must always be smooth, bland, and uniform in taste; they ought never to be greasy, lumpy, or too liquid; the meat constituent should be deliciously tender and wholly in sympathy with the main vegetable ally so that neither dominates but both combine to make a delectable whole that is a triumph of co-operative achievement. A bredie tests the cook's skill not only in blending but also regarding that subtle aptitude, that experience alone can make perfect — to decide when the margin between perfection and over-cooking has been reached.

While all bredies are generically similar, there is a subtle difference in each that accounts for the wide discrepancy in popularity. Some, of course, can be had only when the particular vegetable or fruit which is their basic ingredient is in season; others, again, can be made all the year round. The following are perhaps the most generally known, and all of them are to be found in the oldest recipes. Cabbage bredie, green bean bredie, dried bean bredie, lentil bredie, quince bredie, potato bredie, pumpkin bredie, squash bredie, water-uintjie bredie, sweet-potato bredie, wild cabbage bredies, carrot, parsnip, and turnip bredies, rice bredie, spinach bredie, mielie bredie, turnip or broad-bean tops bredie, cauliflower bredie, brussels sprouts bredie, endive or lettuce bredie, and tomato bredie.

A couple of recipes will show the general technique to be followed in making them.

Potato bredie. Braise in a shallow pot sliced onions, a fragment of garlic, a few coriander seeds, and pepper and salt to taste, with some butter or fat. Add a pound of rib of mutton chopped into pieces about three inches square; the bone must be well trimmed to remove all splinters and the meat must be moderately fat. Add also a small piece of pork or ham, cut into pieces, and let all simmer till nicely browned. Then stir in a pound and a half of par-boiled potatoes, cut into slices, a crushed chilli, if the bredie is to be pungent, or a little lemon juice and a cupful of good stock or white wine. Let the bredie simmer for two to three hours, very slowly, with the lid off the pot. Add stock or water if it becomes too dry. It must be moist without being watery, and all the ingredients must be properly blended.

Tomato bredie. Peel two pounds of ripe tomatoes by plunging them into boiling water and removing the thin skin, and cut them into quarters; add a couple of green ones. Take two pounds of thick rib of mutton, as fat as you

76

can get it; cut it up into neat pieces; dry and dust with meat flour; put into a shallow saucepan with a pound of sliced onions, three sliced leeks or shallots, half an ounce of green ginger, a few cardamons, coriander seeds, peppercorns and fennel seeds, and crushed thyme, marjoram and garlic leaves. If you like the bredie to be hot, add a crushed chilli and plenty of black pepper. Braise all this with sheep fat and when the meat is nicely browned, add the tomatoes; cover closely and let it simmer for several hours, very slowly, shaking frequently. Then add salt to taste, a teaspoonful of chutney sauce and a tablespoonful of moist sugar, and let it simmer for another couple of hours, with the lid off, till it is thickened. Finally add a glass of wine and serve.

Tomato bredie must be a well-spiced tomato puree, surrounding tender bits of meat magnificently impregnated with its flavour. It must not be too watery, and it must never, *never* be greasy, so when the lid is taken off the pot for the open, evaporation cooking for the last couple of hours, all the superabundant fat should be artfully skimmed off, without removing any of the essential gravy. When properly made it is a magnificent dish, always to be served with white rice and boiled potatoes.

Any vegetable can be substituted for potatoes or tomatoes in these recipes; green leaf vegetables, like spinach, are usually pureed before being added to the braised meat. A bredie that is both slightly sweet and sour, is made by adding sorrel leaves and a little extra moist sugar to any vegetable bredie. An interestingly "quaint" dish, as Nash would have described it, is *quince bredie*, made as follows:

Half a dozen ripe quinces; one pound of ribs of mutton cut into small pieces and as fat as you can get it; three large onions; two cloves; a teaspoonful of powdered ginger, a blade of mace, two teaspoonsful of salt, a sprig of rosemary; a little white pepper; half a teacupful of wine; half an ounce of moist sugar. Braise the meat, with all the other ingredients except the quinces (the onions finely sliced) in a little sheep fat; peel the quinces and cut them up into slices without removing the seeds or core; add to the braise and simmer very slowly for three hours or more. Serve with rice and potatoes.

The old fashioned *borrie* quince, with a highly-aromatic flesh, was used for this. A similar bredie was made from apples, pears (especially the monstrous kind that now seems to be extinct) and just-ripe yellow peaches. The combination of meat with a fruit flavour is decidedly attractive. Sometimes a combination of vegetables and fruit was attempted, but such very mixed bredies were not favoured, and the best bredies are unquestionably those in which one principal ingredient is used with the meat. Bredies occupy an anomalous position between vegetable and meat dishes, but are to be regarded as entrees, and are always served with boiled white rice, though some

77

meat cooks on occasion serve yellow rice with them, a change which is welcome when the bredie is very pungent and contains much chilli.

Stuffed or *farced meat* (*gevulde vleis*) is mentioned in the earliest manuscript recipes. Beef was very rarely treated in this way; mutton, pork and game more often, while for poultry it was considered indispensable. A leg or shoulder was taken, the bone removed, the cavity stuffed with one of the farces already described, stitched or skewered up, and the whole was pot roasted, being basted with its own gravy mixed with wine.

This was also a favourite method of cooking ox or sheep's heart, the organ being first boiled in wine, the stuffed whole cut into slices and braised in fat.

Salt or *pickled meat*. The recipes for this are among the oldest we possess, and are relics of the rough domestic cookery of the homelands, gradually modified as taste became more selective. Whatever meat is used, it is first well rubbed with a mixture of salt, salpetre, pepper and coriander seed and is then immersed in a sharp salt-water brine, where it may be left for any length of time. When required for use, it is taken out, well washed and placed in cold fresh water for 24 hours and then boiled — first quickly in water to which a little vinegar has been added, and then more slowly in fresh water with the addition of a bunch of sweet herbs. A few minutes before serving small carrots and turnips are added, and these are served with it. Cold cooked salt or pickled meat may be sliced and fried or grilled or minced according to the various recipes for ham that are given in all the cookery books.

Pork has always been a common and popular meat in South Africa and there are innumerable recipes for preparing it for the table, but few differ in any important point from those with which all European cooks were familiar long before there were any cooks at the Cape. When home-killed it is generally excellent, fat and tender. The sucking pig — which was never of that ideal youth which Lamb would have preferred and was considered in season in spring and not at Christmas — was always baked or pot-roasted, stuffed and served whole. Pork chops were usually cut thick and the best showed a bit of kidney substance; they were grilled, shallow fried, and braised; fillets were always braised or fried, but were held to be ideal when pork was required for any made dish such as a meat pie.

The following is from an old directive:

How to make a good *pork pie*. You must first make the dough for it, for which you want a cupful of fine flour, a lump of butter the size of an egg, two tablespoonsful of the marrow from the bone of an ox, a whole egg and enough fermented must of grape, to which you have added a thimbleful of salt to make a firm paste when you mix it with all the other ingredients. Roll this out several times and then crumple it up and let it stand in a cool place. Then line your dish with a layer of it, keeping some over to cover the meat. For your pie, you take enough pieces of

nice pork, not too fat nor yet too lean, and half their meat number of pieces of some other meat, which you must put in milk and let lie in it for half an hour. Take them out and braise them very lightly in a pan with butter, mace, pepper and salt; then put them in your pie dish with a few hard-boiled eggs cut into slices, a few onion rings, some cloves, a bay leaf and a sprig of lavender; pour over a cupful of wine, cover with the dough, and bake for an hour (or more if you like) in the oven. If you wish it to be coloured outside, rub egg yolk on the dough.

Nowadays one uses baking powder instead of half-fermented must. A spoonful of tapioca added improves the pie which is, however, quite eatable without it.

Poultry, as far as the early cooks were concerned, comprised barnyard fowls, mostly superfluous cocks, ducks and ducklings, of which the muscovy duck was reckoned the choicest, geese, tame pigeons, and, more rarely, turkeys that were never common as they were difficult to rear and when fully-grown were usually tough and tasteless. All these were preferably pot roasted, with spices and herbs and a dash of wine to add to their savour, sometimes larded with pork fat and nearly always appropriately stuffed. Spatchcock grilling was rare; old chickens were usually boiled or stewed, sometimes with elaborate additions.

A few typical recipes will suffice.

Roasted muscovy duck. Truss, trim and rub the carcass inside and out with a clove of garlic. Fill the inside with any stuffing you prefer and sew up tightly. Skewer thin strips of pork fat over the breast and back. Dust with pepper and salt. Put in a pot with sliced onions, pot herbs, a blade of mace and butter or fat. Place on the fire and let it slowly braise, turning the meat over once or twice; then add a cupful of wine, put the lid on, and continue the simmering, putting hot coals on the top of the lid; shake the pot, but do not lift the lid. The simmering must be gentle; so must the shaking for the bird must be firm and whole when it is served. When it is quite tender, which takes a couple of hours at least, put it on the dish in which it is to be served and drip lemon juice over it. Thicken the gravy with a little brown roux, adding salt if required, and serve separately in a sauce boat.

Stewed fowl. If the fowl is old, let it hang for a couple of days after it has been cleaned. Cut it into neat pieces; flour them and put them into a fireproof dish with a well fitting cover; add a bunch of pot herbs, a blade of mace, peppercorns, and a handful of small onions, peeled and cut in halves, and a cup of white wine. Cover the dish and place it in the oven for a few hours; then let it get cold, add some more wine, salt to taste, and replace it in the oven for another slow stewing for at least three hours. Take out the pieces, and put them on the serving dish; beat up the yolk of a fresh egg with a tablespoonful of tamarind water (or lemon juice); stir it into the gravy and let it thicken but not boil; pour over the fowl and serve.

79

meat Some old recipes add vermicelli or tapioca; some allspice, and one even mentions chillies; but poultry does not take kindly, when boiled, to the sharp pungency of Spanish pepper. Pigeons stewed in this way are delicious, but they need larding; so does a turkey. A goose, on the other hand, is generally fat enough to do without additional lubrication and is best pot roasted, with an appropriate stuffing. Both it and the muscovy duck, when so roasted, are sent to the table accompanied by their livers, fried in butter with a little salt and pepper, of which each guest receives a small portion as a special tit-bit.

Chapter VII

MORE MEAT DISHES

ON the farms, when domestic animals were slaughtered, no part of the animal was discarded; what could not be used for food, was useful in some other way. The old recipes paid due attention to the preparation of *afval*, which literally means "cast offings", but include not only tripe, but such organs as the heart, kidneys, liver, sweetbreads and certain other glands, as well as "butchers' pieces" like trotters, feet, heads, tongues and ears. As it was a common custom to kill more than one animal at a time, there was ample opportunity to combine different meats and convert all the scraps from the various carcases into wholesome food.

One of the best known and most popular, as well as one of the most tasty dishes, was

Pig's brawn (vark sult). Take the pig's head and split it; take also the feet and tail; clean them all thoroughly; strew salt over and let them stand in a cool place overnight. The next day rub them lightly with a mixture of salt and salpetre and let them again abide for a night in a cool place. Then place them in a saucepan with cold water and let them remain in it for a couple of hours; take them out and put them in another saucepan with enough water to cover them; boil till the flesh easily strips from the bone; pour through a sieve, and let the liquid remain warm on the stove; sort the meat from the bones; put the bones back into the liquid; skin the tongue and put the skin, with the pig's ears, also back into the liquid, which must slowly simmer. Cut up the tongue and all the meat into small pieces. Strain the soup and reject what remains in the

meat sieve. Put the liquid back in the saucepan, add the tongue and meat, mace, a couple of laurel leaves, grated nutmeg, pepper and salt; boil till it begins to thicken; then add a cup of good vinegar or of tamarind water; pour into moulds. Serve cold.

Some recipes recommend the addition of turmeric or curry powder; some add saffron, which agreeably varies both the taste and the colour. The brawn should be moderately stiff, variegated in appearance, piquantly sour and with the flavour of a strong jellied consommé.

Pannas, that like *tassal* really has no English name, is a modification of a dish that was known to the Avignon cooks in the fifteenth century. It is referred to by old travellers as "a greasy blood pudding, or haggis, badly fried", but when well made is nothing of the sort, although its taste may have to be acquired. Here it is:

The liver and kidneys of the pig to be cleaned of all skin and gristle, cut into bits and lightly fried; then to be pounded in the mortar, with breadcrumbs, pepper and salt and a teaspoonful of fennel seed; then to be mixed thoroughly with enough blood to make a paste, to which you add enough tamarind water to sour it slightly, and put it in a flat pan, smeared with fat, and bake it in the oven. When it is baked, pour butter, melted, over it, and you can keep it for several weeks. To use it, you take it out of the pan, slice it and fry the slices in fat. If you like, you may strew parsley over it before it goes to the table.

An excellent breakfast dish, but the recipe omits something it should have mentioned — tiny bits of pork fat that should be incorporated in the paste; they add greatly to its savouriness.

An old recipe for *marrow pudding:*

Put in a lubricated pudding dish a layer of white crumbs previously soaked in milk, from which the moisture has been pressed; put on it the marrow from the bone of an ox, a few chopped almonds, blanched, and a few walnuts and flavour with salt, pepper, nutmeg and a scraping of lemon peel. Fill the mould in this way with two or three layers, with a bread layer on top. Make a sauce with egg yolk, butter and milk; salt it and pour it over the pudding. Tie a cloth over it, place the mould in a large saucepan and steam it for an hour. Turn out and serve with a sour sauce.

Here is one for *kidneys in potatoes:*

Take a couple of calf's kidneys and four pig's kidneys; clean them and remove all membrane vessels and hard bits; chop them up and braise them in butter with some parsley, grated nutmeg, lemon rind, pepper and salt; bake large potatoes in their skin in the oven, and when they are soft, divide each carefully, without breaking them, length-wise; scoop out a hollow in each half and fill with the braised kidney; put the two halves together and tie with a thread; put in the oven to get thoroughly hot and serve.

Liver was always a highly-popular part of the animal and **meat** was supposed to have health-giving qualities, a presumption that is thoroughly warranted. There are many ways of preparing it, most of them simply variants of recognised European recipes. It was grilled over the coals, larded and braised with tomatoes (a comparatively late recipe), onions or aubergines, made into patties and puddings, steamed or fried, stewed with or without additions, and served with curry sauce. One recipe is peculiar in that it mentions a particular kind of liver, and may be quoted, although it properly belongs to the next chapter:

Creamed liver. Take of the liver of a muscovy duck, or of a goose or fowl or, which is best of all, of a flamingo, half a pound; wash and dry it, and strew salt and fine pepper over it. Put in a deep pie dish, buttered, a layer of sliced onions and parsnips; lay the liver on top of this and cover it with a layer of breadcrumbs; pour over a cupful of thin, sour cream; put in the oven and let it bake. Take boiled rice and mix it with chopped parsley, cloves, pepper and salt. Put it in a pan with plenty of butter and heat it till the rice has absorbed all the butter, adding some strong stock to keep it moist; put the rice in a dish, pile the stewed liver on it and cover with the cream sauce.

Ham figures extensively in the recipes. It was cured according to the age-old methods employed in Europe, but was rarely eaten raw and more often boiled or baked and, as a breakfast dish, fried with eggs.

Baked ham. Place it in cold water for several hours, and then plunge it into boiling water; as soon as the water again boils, take it out and place it in another saucepan. Cover it with a mixture of wine and vinegar, and whatever spice and herbs you fancy, and boil it slowly till it is done. Then take it out; wipe it dry, and cover it with a paste made of honey and flour, after you have first skinned it neatly. Stick into it as many cloves as you wish, and bake it in a shallow pan in the oven, pouring over it wine, and basting it frequently with the gravy. Serve cold or hot as you please.

Tongue, both sheep's and ox-tongue, was always boiled or parboiled before being served; it was never dried, but frequently pickled or salted and was always regarded as a delicate dish. A fresh boiled ox tongue was not usually skinned, but when served cold or pickled, skinning was a usual preliminary, and the meat was allowed to jelly in the liquid in which it had been boiled.

Stewed tongue. Cut a cooked fresh or salt tongue into thick slices; rub into them sage, marjoram, pounded coriander seed, salt and pepper; braise a few onion slices in butter; put in the tongue and pour over it a little rum. Let it simmer gently, shaking the pan frequently so that the meat absorbs as much of the juice as possible; serve on fried bread, with a dusting of parsley.

meat *Sheep's tongue with celery.* Take half a dozen sheep tongues; clean and trim them. Put them in a stewpot with a cup of wine, the white part of six young celery shoots, a few young onions chopped up, a blade of mace, grated nutmeg and pepper and salt. Cover closely and simmer, shaking frequently. When the tongues are soft, add a large lump of butter, a tablespoonful of lemon juice and a handful of young carrots; stew for not longer than ten minutes and serve.

The carrots should be just parboiled, retaining all their crispness; a chilled sambal is served with the dish, which is really a combination of braised celery and stewed tongue.

Tongue bobotie. Take cooked pig's and sheep tongues; skin and pound them to a paste; mix with it the yolk of two eggs, a crushed chilli, a bay leaf, half a dozen allspice, a few coriander seeds, a teaspoonful of rum, a tablespoonful of tamarind water in which you have mixed some turmeric powder, and half a cupful of coconut milk, with salt and pepper to taste. Pour over it a mixture of egg yolk and cream, mixed with a little turmeric powder; stick a few blanched almonds on top and bake in the oven.

This is much improved if pounded almonds are incorporated in the paste. It is served with boiled rice, sambals and chutney.

Ox and sheeps hearts were always stuffed, parboiled and then braised with onions, spices, herbs and a little rum or wine, after having been cut in moderately thin slices. An interesting, and to strangers impressive, modification was to stuff them with an almond farce, stew them lightly in white wine, and serve with a white sauce, appropriately spiced. Another variation was to fry the slices, previously stuffed, in batter. A third was to mince the cooked hearts and to braise the mince with onions, spices and herbs and fill small pancakes with them, serving these with a sour white sauce. A later recipe directs that they be stewed in white wine, with grated pineapple, with the usual spice flavourings, covered with tart dough and baked in the oven – a modified kind of *dariole* that was popular about the middle of the past century, but is now no longer fashionable although it is well worth eating.

Brains and sweetbreads were lightly parboiled, and then stewed, with spices, herbs, a few drops of rum, or fried by themselves or with the addition of spices, breadcrumbs, and herbs. Sometimes they were fried in batter; less often they were braised with vegetables into a ragout. Gently steamed in white wine, with the addition of salt, pepper and nutmeg, they were esteemed as a dish for invalids.

A dish which although not peculiar to the Cape – as it is mentioned in the early Italian cookery books that date from the sixteenth century – is one that was common enough a hundred years ago but is nowadays never mentioned. When young rams were castrated, the genital glands were available for culinary use and were prepared for the table in exactly the same way as were sweetbreads.

84

They were shallow-fried, braised with garlic and onion **meat** and herbs and spices, stewed in butter and wine, or fried in batter, and were regarded as a great delicacy. Two recipes for the preparation of "A ragout of lamb's-stones" and "A lamb-stone stew" are given in Mrs Rundle's *Domestic Cookery* published in 1827, and are obviously transcripts from a manuscript Cape cookery book. As it is now practically impossible to obtain the material for this dish, except for those who live on a farm, it is not necessary to give directions for its preparation, and the curious are referred to the printed work mentioned.

It may be said that the ragout is a delicate and intriguing dish that certainly merits a gourmet's attention.

Trotters, that apparently consist merely of tough sinews and bone, were extensively used — not only for brawn, for which both pig's and sheep's trotters were employed, and for jelly, for which sheep's and calf's feet served, but also for several attractive dishes in which the cook had an opportunity to show skill and artistry. The old recipes lay great emphasis on the desirability of keeping the "oil" that came from boiling the tendons and bones: it was skimmed off and preserved in jars, and was in great demand as a salad and toilet oil.

Stewed trotters. For this you want half a dozen pig's or sheep's feet, which you must carefully clean, scrape and wash well in salt water. Cut them up into pieces and boil them in salt water till the flesh comes off the bone; skim off the fat which you may use in other ways. Take the flesh and put it into a shallow pot with three large onions sliced, a blade of mace, a sprig of rosemary or the top leaves of a sprig of mint, some pepper and some salt and a few tablespoonsful of wine; stew gently for half an hour and add some breadcrumbs; stir well and let it stand for a few moments; then whisk in a couple of egg yolks beaten up with the juice of a large lemon; serve at once with a grating of nutmeg over all.

An attractive dish; the addition of a pittosporum leaf is an important improvement; so is the help of a few spoonsful of cream.

There are recipes for currying them, serving them with a cheese sauce, in batter, pickling them and simply sauteeing them in butter. They may even be stuffed by a skilled cook, though the result is not always what it should be. Cold they make an excellent salad and in a pie they lend an enticing blandness to the contents.

There is perhaps no foodstuff that in English cookery books is treated so scurvily as *tripe*. Its nutritive value is high and, properly prepared, it makes a delicate and tender dish. Most of the recipes at the Cape are undoubtedly echoes from the cookery of the south of France, where the methods of cooking tripe are almost as numerous as the sauces that may be served with it. They have, of course, undergone modifications here, as the following recipes show:

85

meat *Stewed tripe.* Soak it in salt water; then clean it thoroughly; wash in fresh water and beat it with a wooden mallet, but not enough to wound it. Cut up into small pieces; put these in a stew pot with some bits of fat pork, a couple of lemon leaves, a large piece of mace, some sliced onions, white pepper and salt; cover with white wine, and let it boil slowly for several hours till the meat is quite tender, adding wine to make up for what evaporates. When tender, let it simmer till the liquid has been reduced to half, taking care that the meat does not burn. Add a cup of cream mixed with a tablespoonful of lemon juice; thicken with rice flour and serve with grated nutmeg.

Baked tripe with tangerine peel. Boil the tripe, cut in small strips, in white wine or stock. When tender, take out the pieces and put them in a buttered pie dish. Take some of the liquid in which it has been boiled; add to it a large lump of butter, a teaspoonful of grated nutmeg, a teaspoonful of pounded tangerine peel, a teaspoonful of Chinese (soya) sauce, the juice of half a lemon, a little pepper and salt to savour, boil it up, mix it with some breadcrumbs, and pour it over the tripe. Strew breadcrumbs over, dot with bits of butter, and bake in the oven.

Buttermilk tripe. Cook the tripe in buttermilk till it is quite tender (a good way to do this is to place it with the milk in a jar with a closely fitting lid, and put the jar in a saucepan of boiling water, where it must remain for the whole night boiling slowly). It will need at least several hours to boil perfectly tender, and you must add milk from time to time, bringing it to the boil again after each addition. When done, add some parsley, grated lemon peel, pepper, salt and either some blades of mace or cloves, whichever you prefer. Boil again for half an hour, and then take out the tripe, put in it your dish, and pour over what remains of the buttermilk – to which you have added a large lump of butter and a cupful of good thick cream beaten up with the yolk of an egg and a glass of rum or brandy. Serve with a little grated nutmeg over.

Quince tripe. Cook the tripe, cut into pieces, in wine with a little salt and pepper till it is quite tender; take out the pieces and put them in a fireproof dish, with sliced ripe quinces, a powdering of ginger, a few cloves, and some salt; moisten with some wine and lemon juice mixed and put in the oven till the quinces are soft; beat up a couple of egg yolks with thin cream and melted butter, add a little rice flour and salt, stir into the dish and bake till it has set. Grate a little nutmeg over it, and serve.

Fried tripe. Take pieces of cooked tripe, selecting the thickest; dip them in a thin batter made by mixing an egg yolk with sifted flour and a little milk, to which you have added salt and a pinch of powdered chilli (cayenne pepper) and fry them in fat or butter. Pile the pieces on a dish and strew parsley over and serve.

Tripe and sheep's head (kop en pootjies). For this you

86

want not only sheep's tripe, but also the head of the sheep meat and the trotters. Clean all three well and cut up the tripe into small pieces. Put the head and trotters in a saucepan, with some onions, a bunch of herbs, salt and pepper, and boil till the flesh easily separates from the bones. Take the flesh and the pieces of tripe in a stewpot with pepper and salt, a blade of mace, a lemon leaf, a little grated nutmeg, a wineglassful of lemon juice and two cups of strong stock; let it boil up, then simmer gently till the liquid part is thickened. Serve with chopped parsley. This dish is varied by adding curry powder, in which case it becomes a jellied curry, or by thickening with cream, tapioca, or vermicelli.

Oxtail is generally stewed or braised, always with a good wine and spices and herbs as an appropriate addition. *Ox marrow* is baked in the oven, the bone being cut into short lengths and both ends closed with a pat of dough. It is served with bread and eaten with a little salt and pepper or, more rarely, with a sweet mustard, made with plenty of sugar and cream and butter.

South African *biltong*, which is really spiced dried meat, is made from beef or from game meat. In the former case it is always cut into exceedingly thin slices and eaten on bread and butter; in the latter it is generally grated or pounded and is always dry, whereas beef biltong should be moist with a modicum of fat attached to it. Beef biltong, cut slightly thicker, is also fried like a bacon rasher or grilled, and is then served with fried eggs. Another name for biltong, often used in the older recipes is *tassal* in which, however, the meat was generally cut into small strips as is now done with game biltong.

Beef biltong. Take a good-sized piece (18 or 24 inches long) of the inner back muscle, or of the thigh muscle, selecting a nicely rounded strip, about six inches in diameter. It must not have any tendon, but should have some fat, though not too much. Trim it into an even, elongated oval. Make a mixture of salt, pepper, salpetre, crushed coriander and fennel seed and moisten it with vinegar; rub this into the meat, and cover the meat with it for a few days, rubbing the mixture in every day. Hang the biltong in a draught and continue the rubbing with the spicy mixture

87

meat till the outside is wind-dry. Tie a cheese cloth round it and hang it in a chimney for a couple of weeks to get thoroughly smoked. Keep it in a cool place, and use it when you have need for it.

Some makers put the biltong in a brine for a couple of days, and then start the rubbing process. Whichever method is used, the result should be a dark-coloured, firm, elongated piece of dried meat, which cuts easily and when sliced is a tender, garnet red segment, surrounded by a thin, more darkly covered integument that need never be pared off before eating. Its taste is deliciously spicy, and whatever bits of fat remain in or on it are agreeably soft, without any suspicion of rancidity. If it has been hung in the smoke of a wood fire, it has that added aromatic flavour that is so difficult to describe yet so characteristic of smoked meat.

Game biltong as made in the field is quite another thing. It is simply game meat, cut into thin strips, rubbed with salt and perhaps a little crushed coriander seed, and sun-dried in the open air till it is as hard as a board. Bits of it are cut off with a pocket knife and chewed by those whose teeth are strong enough for such manducation, or are roughly pounded to a loose, grey mass that can be mastered even by those who have to rely on their dentures. The best way of serving game biltong is to grate it on a grater or rasp it with a broad rasp; the resultant powder, which should be greyish red, is spread on thin bread and butter. Biltong is an extremely nutritious and a most easily digested food, and can be given safely to invalids, while it is a deliciously savoury filling for sandwiches. As it is always made from lean meat, it should be eaten with butter. Practically any game meat can be used for it, but the best kind is reputed to be that made from the flesh of the eland or the riet buck. I have tasted good biltong made from lion's meat and, most excellent of all, from zebra meat. All game biltong, however, can be much improved if it is made with the addition of some aromatic spices to the salt with which it is rubbed before being dried.

It is so excellent by itself that it needs no embellishment. Nevertheless it makes an excellent sandwich filling, mixed with butter and a few drops of onion or lemon juice. It is also a food companion to certain egg dishes, like shirred, scrambled and poached eggs. A little-known way of using it is to incorporate it in an egg and milk and cream custard which is baked in the oven.

88

Chapter VIII

SAUCES AND SALAD DRESSINGS

THE dictionaries define sauce as "a liquid relish for food"; etymologists derive the word from the Latin word *salsa* which is supposed to mean a saltish fluid, but Von Vaerst thinks that it is of Eastern derivation. What can be stated as fact is that the old Roman cooks never called their sauce a *salsa*. Apicius, one of the first writers on cookery, speaks of *salso* by which, apparently, he means a salty addition to a wine, for in his time it was customary to dilute table wine with sea water. Pliny and Cato refer to *salsugo*, and as the latter states that it may be thickened with *amylum*, which is ordinary starch, it is likely that it corresponded to a made sauce. Roman cooks used as a relish for all their meat and fish dishes something they called *jus*, which was the juice or gravy in which the foodstuff was prepared. The French cooks gave us the word sauce for the combinations of such juices with cream, oil and various other ingredients. In old Cape recipes the word *sous* is used indiscriminately for such made-up sauce, for gravy (for which Dutch cooks use the word *jus*) and for whatever remains liquid in the stew-pan, while uncooked juice of fruit or vegetables is termed *sap*.

Obviously the preparation of an elaborate sauce represents a sophistication of the art of cookery to which the early Cape cooks had not attained. Their first examples of such sauces were made from Oriental recipes, and were cooked sauces. Raw sauces, which are more correctly

89

sauces speaking dressings, were used – but there were few, the principal one being *sour sauce*, made by beating up an egg with vinegar, salt and pepper. One reason for this was the scarcity of vegetable oil, which had to be brought from Europe or Java. Even today South Africa, which has many indigenous oil holding plants, does not produce enough vegetable oil for domestic use, although a small quantity of excellent cold-drawn olive oil is seasonally made in the Cape Province.

Oil for saucemaking purposes was usually extracted from fats. A favourite oil for such use was that skimmed off in the first boiling of trotters or meat containing tendons or fat; this was clarified, put into bottles and used when required. Coconut oil, brought from the East, was also sometimes used and, after the eighteenth century, various seed oils, also imported.

According to Kettner there are two basic sauces, one white and the other brown, that masquerade under various names, but are generically known as white sauce and Spanish sauce. The difference between them is that the first is essentially a cooked sauce, while in the second the flour has been braised. Both were known to the old Cape cooks, and recipes for them are indeed to be found in the oldest cookery books. The Cape method of preparation directs that a very strong broth should be made, mainly of veal and chicken, boiled in good bouillon to which has been added a sliced onion, a bunch of carrots, a bouquet of pot herbs, pepper, salt and a little sugar. The fat should be carefully skimmed off. The broth is then strained through a cloth, and replaced in the saucepan. In another saucepan a cup of butter is melted and half a cup of sifted flour is stirred into it, till it is a smooth paste, which is then stirred into the broth, which is boiled under constant stirring. As soos as this boils, it is drawn to a cooler place on the stove, and allowed to simmer gently till it is smooth and thick. It is then poured through a fine sieve, and is ready to be used either as a sauce by itself, or as the basis for other sauces.

Thus, beaten up with an equal quantity of nearly boiling cream, it becomes bechamel sauce which again, when mixed with a jellied chicken broth and allowed to cool, becomes cold bechamel sauce. The gamut of variations is almost endless, as may be seen from consulting any good modern cookery book. None of these sauces, made with such basic velvet sauce, is original in Cape cookery. The earliest variant of the brown variety is the following:

Brown sauce (bruin sous). Place in a saucepan a layer of sliced onions, with a tablespoonful of sheep's tail fat; put on it a pound each of beef and veal, cut up into sizeable pieces. Pour on two cups of water and let it boil till most of the water has boiled away and the broth is thick enough "to cling to the side of the pot". Take great care that it does not burn. Now add four cups of boiling water and put the pot on a cooler part of the stove where it can simmer gently; add a little salt, and skim; then add carrots, parsley,

90

a bunch of celery, a few cloves, a blade of mace and a pinch of black pepper. Let it simmer gently for four hours or more; then pour through a sieve and mix with brown roux to the required consistency.

This is not different from the usual recipes in European cookery books, except for the addition of the mace and cloves that impart to the sauce a spicy piquancy. Like the velvet sauce, it is used both as a basis for other sauces and by itself. The most common addition, in early times, was a teaspoonful of China (soya) sauce, or of a sharp chilli sauce. The following made-sauces required no foundation sauce but were complete in themselves:

Quince sauce. Bake the quinces; peel them when they are soft and remove the seeds. Beat them with a wooden spoon to a puree; add salt, a little powdered ginger, tangerine peel and white pepper; rub through a fine sieve, and dilute with a little lemon juice.

Apple and pear sauce was made in the same way, but usually a few drops of rum were added.

Oil sauce (used for brawn and salt meat). Mix oil and vinegar in equal proportions, with salt, pepper, a little moist brown sugar and the expressed juice of an orange; beat well and serve cold.

Celery sauce. Braise white celery shoots cut into small pieces in butter with a little onion, pepper, salt and sugar; when tender, stir in some sifted flour, add a cupful of milk and let it simmer till thick; pour through a sieve and serve very hot.

Cape gooseberry sauce (appelliefiesous). Boil the gooseberries in water; when tender take them out and press through a sieve; add to the puree a large lump of butter, a little sugar and, if you like, a pinch of powdered ginger and a teaspoonful of salt; put on the fire and beat constantly, adding a little white wine while you are whipping it, but do not let it boil. It may be coloured yellow by adding a little turmeric. It should be sour-sweet; if you wish it to be sharply sour, cook some unripe grapes with the berries.

Several kinds of fruit — loquats, green grapes, cherries and strawberries — were similarly treated to make a fruit sauce. A very pleasant-tasting and smooth fruit sauce was made from the berries of the *duinbessie* (*muraltia spinosa*) that grew abundantly on Green Point Common and could be obtained, when in season, on the market for a penny a pound. Duneberry sauce had a sharp, sweet-sour taste and an intriguing, aromatic flavour, and was excellent with all meat dishes.

Pork fat sauce (speksous) was made from slightly salted, but not cured, pork fat, which was cut into tiny pieces, and

sauces braised with pepper and salt, a pinch of powdered chilli and a few crushed sage leaves. A tablespoonful of sifted flour was mixed to a paste with wine or water, and stirred into a cup of water mixed with vinegar in which the yolks of three eggs had been whipped. When the pork was nicely browned, the mixture of flour, egg yolk and vinegar was stirred into it, and was allowed to simmer gently till the sauce was smoothly thickened. It was used both hot and cold.

Old fashioned sauce. This was the *ousous* of some recipes; *rissiesous* of others. It was made as follows:

Pound two peeled onions in the mortar with three green chillies, salt and a couple of tablespoonsful of the flesh of a braised bokkom (dried herring or mullet). Braise this puree with plenty of butter; add a few tablespoonsful of a mild *blatjang* (fruit chilli sauce; later recipes substitute for it tomato sauce) and thin, if required, with stock or white sauce.

Sour sauce. Melt an ounce of salt butter and whip into it the yolks of two eggs, the sap of a large lemon, a pinch of white pepper and a cup of boiled cream. Put on the fire, whipping constantly, and let it thicken, but take care that it does not boil. Some recipes add vinegar or tamarind water, but the lemon juice should sour it sufficiently; it should never be a sharp sauce.

Burnt almond sauce. Burnt almonds are pounded and mixed with a butter sauce, with sugar, lemon juice, and enough red ochre (*rooi bolus*) to colour the sauce bright red. Finally a glass of very sweet wine or of home-made liqueur is added. It is a favourite sauce for steamed puddings, but can be served also with meat dishes.

Moskonfytsous has for its main ingredients the boiled, partly-fermented wine must known as *moskonfyt*, which is simply grape juice in which the sugar has been largely, though not wholly, caramelised. By itself moskonfyt, which was well known to the ancient Romans who also used it as a sweet sauce, is a dark mahogany-coloured thin syrup, with a vinous yet aromatic flavour combined with the distinct, characteristic taste of burnt sugar. It is commonly used by itself as a syrup with bread and butter at breakfast and, commercially, as a sweetening agent for fortified wines of the port type. As a sauce principally for puddings and sweet dishes and, more rarely, for meat dishes, it is thickened with arrowroot, rice flour, or sifted wheat flour, mixed with well-chopped seeded raisins, dates and some chilli sauce to give it additional pungency. In that way it becomes one of the many sweet sauces, of which there are innumerable varieties that need not be detailed here. Reference will be made in a later chapter to some of them.

Klipkoussous, made by mixing finely-pounded braised or stewed flesh of the pearl mussel with a basic white or

velvet sauce, always needs the addition of lemon juice, **sauces**
egg yolk and spices. It is a delicately-flavoured sauce
which, like all sauces that contain fish, has a distinct and
rather an esoteric taste. Like crayfish sauce, in which the
principal ingredient is the coral and the very soft parts
found under the carapace, and oyster sauce, it is usually
served with fish dishes.

Herb sauces, of which the best known to European
cooks are mint and sage sauce, are made either plainly
by boiling the chief constituent in vinegar, with sugar and
some spice that will not overpower the characteristic
flavour of the herb, or by combining the herbs with other
ingredients. As an example of an old fashioned sauce of
this kind the following recipe will serve:

Fennel sauce. Take a handful of young fennel leaves
and chop them up fine, with a little parsley, salt and pepper,
and the yolk of a hard-boiled egg pressed through a sieve.
Make an emulsion of oil, lemon juice and vinegar, and
whip it up with the fennel mixture, adding a little ground
ginger if desired. Serve with fish. It was regarded as the
sauce for an eel pie, and was also favoured as a relish for
all firm-fleshed fish.

A sauce that is of ancient date but is now rarely en-
countered, is

Saffron sauce. Braise sliced onions, shallots, and a tiny
morsel of garlic in butter; add to it the pounded flesh of a
baked quince or apple, a pinch of powdered saffron, a
large lump of salt butter and a little white stock; let it
slowly simmer; press through a sieve, add another lump of
butter, and let it get thoroughly hot again, without boiling.
It should be uniformly bright yellow in colour and quite
smooth. Some recipes thicken it with a little rice flour.

The Malay cooks were adepts at making the exceedingly
pungent, sharp, well-spiced sauces that are so much
favoured in the East. They vary in consistency from the
thick, jammy chutneys to the thinner, more liquid combinations of spices and other ingredients with tamarind or
vinegar, professionally known as *blatjangs*. Sometimes
the latter were made with a fish paste and with partly
fermented, even decomposed, materials that gave a very
strong, and often, to Occidental taste at least, a repulsive
odour. An example of such a strongly flavoured and
odoriferous sauce is the Malay *trassie*, a variant of which
was apparently regarded as a delicacy by the early
Romans who made it from decomposed anchovies. More
in keeping with modern palates are the following recipes:

Fish trassie. Pound to a paste in a mortar six anchovies,
a dried salt mullet, three red chillies, a slice of ginger, half a
dozen pepper corns, a teaspoonful of coriander and the
same amount of aniseed. Braise in butter half a cupful of
chopped onion and a small clove of garlic; pour over it a
cupful of tamarind water, mix it with the fish paste, and

sauces let it slowly simmer, keeping the lid on the saucepan till all ingredients have been well cooked, adding more tamarind water or vinegar to make a pasty fluid. Put in bottles and cork.

This is a fiery sauce, which keeps well, and is without the nauseating odour of the true *trassie* that is made from decomposed fish.

Hot blatjang. Take a pound of dried apricots and soak them in vinegar till they are soft enough to be mashed. Peel two pounds of onions, bake them, and pound them, with the mashed apricots, to a smooth puree, in which you incorporate a quarter of a pound of salt, half an ounce of coriander seed, half a pound of chopped green chillies, two large cloves of garlic, a teaspoonful of powdered ginger, and half a pound of blanched almonds previously well pounded. Put in a saucepan six pints of vinegar and bring it to the boil; add your paste, stirring constantly, and let it simmer till it reaches the thickness you wish it to have. Put in bottles or jars and cork. It will keep indefinitely.

Blatjang should be a uniform red colour, and it is better to use red, that is mature, chillies, but the green ones make a more pungent relish. This recipe gives a blatjang that is scaldingly hot and should be used cautiously by those who are unfamiliar with its properties. By adding sugar, or apricot jam, to it, decreasing the amount of chillies or omitting them altogether and substituting ordinary pepper, a sweet blatjang can be made according to this recipe. There are many other recipes for making this favourite condiment, but the essentials are that it should be bitingly spicy, pungently aromatic, moderately smooth and a very intimately mixed association of all the ingredients.

Atjar, another favourite relish, is simply a variety of vegetables and fruits, boiled and preserved in a very strong chilli pickle. The more varieties of vegetables in it, the better it is supposed to be. An old recipe states:

For *atjar* you must take small onions, shallots, cauliflower, very young mielie (corn) cobs, green beans, half ripe apricots, very small immature cucumbers, squashes and pumpkins, not more than two inches in length, and not thicker than your little finger, ripe loquats from which you have removed the seeds, one or two half-ripe rose apples (*djam boes*), dried peeled peaches, a few green and red chillies, some lemon leaves, some green ginger diced, peppercorns, curry powder, moist sugar, salt and vinegar. After cleaning your vegetables and fruit, you must put them in the vinegar and boil them till they are soft; then you must make a paste with the sugar, salt and curry powder, and stir it into the boiling vinegar, adding the peppercorns, chillies and lemon leaves, and let it all boil sweetly till the liquid begins to thicken. Now put it in jars and tie a vinegar-wetted cloth over, and let it stand for a week or two when you can eat it as a pickle with meat.

94

A well-made atjar is an enthralling relish, for you never **sauces** know, when you are fishing in the jar, what you may come across – and every bit is as enticing as a good vegetable pickle can be. Some cooks add too much sugar and make it too sweet; it should be pleasantly sour, with a sweetish aftertaste, and every constituent should be deliciously tender. Perhaps the titbit in it is the young mielie cobs, each encrusted with its serried rows of unripened grain, but there is really no end to the variety of things you can incorporate in it.

Chutneys are sour-sweet, hot-sweet, or simply sweet concoctions of fruits or vegetables with spices and vinegar; their sweetness depends on the amount of sugar (formerly honey) that was added to them; their fieriness they owe to the pepper and chillies that go into them. Formerly they were all made at home; now they are usually bought ready-made by mass production, and are far from being what they ought to be.

There are many recipes for making them, but it would obviously be monotonous to transcribe so many whose generic similarity is obvious. I have been served with apricot chutney, almond chutney, made from green almonds, bean chutney, mango chutney, pineapple chutney, roseapple chutney, cucumber chutney, melon chutney, bean chutney, apple chutney, quince chutney (perhaps the best of all), peach chutney, plum chutney, pumpkin chutney, mielie chutney, made from small, immature cobs, pear chutney, grape chutney, kei apple chutney, kaffir plum chutney (both made from indigenous fruits), raisin chutney, mixed dried fruit chutney and last, and very definitely, least, the modern tomato chutney, which is not really a chutney, but a sauce. For chutney should be essentially a preserve, in which the consistency of the main ingredient, that gives a name to it, should be maintained and something of its original form should remain. Tomatoes do not figure in the old recipes, for

95

sauces they were a comparatively late introduction, but when they were freely grown a tomato chutney was made and it is a delicious chutney. It was prepared from young, unripe tomatoes, stewed with sugar, spice and tamarind juice, and was quite unlike the modern watery red concoction that consists of ripe tomato mash, boiled up with sugar, raisins and what passes for vinegar.

The following two recipes describe how, generally speaking, a chutney should be made:

Quince chutney. Take two dozen borrie quinces, just ripe; peel and slice but do not core them, for the gelatinous seeds add much to the flavour of the chutney. Cook them till soft in white wine. Now add to them six or seven cloves of garlic, bruised, and two pounds of moist sugar, and let them simmer. Pound in a mortar a pound of young onions, peeled and sliced, half a pound of dried chillies, a pound of seeded hanepoot raisins, a quarter of a pound of green ginger, a teaspoonful of cardamons, allspice, and pepper, and a tablespoonful of tangerine peel, and add this to the quinces; pour over three bottles of good wine vinegar or tamarind water, and let it come to the boil, stirring constantly. Let the chutney simmer till it is of the right consistency, taking care that the quince slices retain their shape. Put in wide-mouthed jars. It will keep indefinitely.

Rose apple chutney. Boil the rose apples in wine till they are soft; remove their seeds. Make a paste of onion, fennel seed, coriander seed, garlic, cloves, moist sugar and ginger powder, and stir this into boiling vinegar; let it simmer, and add pounded raisins and dates, chillies enough to make the chutney very hot, and half a cupful of salt; put into it your boiled rose apples, and let all simmer slowly for three hours, taking care that it does not burn.

This is a delicious chutney, for the strong flavour of the rose apples is predominant. It was usually far too strong, however, for delicate palates, but its fieriness can of course be moderated by using little or no chillies. Let me again emphasise that a real chutney is not a sauce but a soursweet preserve, in which the main ingredient retains its pristine shape, or as much of it as possible, for in one or two recipes – for apple and pumpkin chutney and, more especially, for the many mixed fruit chutneys – it is directed that the fruit or the vegetable should be mashed. Such chutneys are, however, more properly described as thick fruit or vegetable sauces and are more in the nature of a blatjang than a real chutney.

We now come to *salads*. Here again there is considerable difference of opinion about the derivation of the word and its original meaning, matters with which we need not concern ourselves at the moment. The word *slaai* which is Dutch, and the word *sambal* which is Malay, are interchangeably used in the old recipes to denote a cold meat, vegetable or fruit dish, garnished with a cold dressing, and served sometimes by itself but more often as an accompaniment of some other dish. The meat and

96

fish salads were copied from recipes that occur in the oldest cookery books and, as far as I have been able to ascertain, none of them shows any modification (apart from the inclusion of some ingredients that are indigenous to the country) that can be considered an original improvement. Any cold meat or fish could be served up as a salad. The meat was simply sliced into small, convenient pieces, mixed with sliced onions and fresh herbs or salad vegetables, dressed with a sour sauce, and served with appropriate decorative garnishes.

At the Cape, the dressing was generally the yolk of an egg beaten with vinegar or sour cream, with salt, pepper and perhaps some powdered chilli added. A mayonnaise sauce was a late introduction, for oil, as has been mentioned, was rare; on the farms one very seldom came across an oil dressing for a salad. For the decorative garnishing hard boiled eggs, cut into thin slices (I have seen hard boiled ostrich eggs used for this purpose), boiled beetroot, and pickles were generally used. In more fashionable homes in the towns nuts, anchovies and, for sweet salads, preserved ginger, citron, shaddock and naartjie or rose-apple preserve were used to dress it up.

No recipes for meat and fish salads need be given; they are to be found in all cookery books. The only noticeable hint I have discovered in the old Cape recipes is that in hussar salad, if made in the early summer, the inclusion of a few slices of ripe figs is a decided improvement. An interesting, though not novel, modification in chicken salad (which all the best recipes insist should be made from the breast flesh alone) is the addition of a few drops of rum, the directive being: "Before adding the sauce, put a few drops of a good rum on the pieces of chicken and toss them about so that each piece gets a touch of it." Rum as a flavouring for meat is nothing new, but its use in so delicate a dish as a chicken salad is to be carefully controlled, and I cannot say that my own experience with it has convinced me that it improves the dish.

Crayfish, crab and shellfish salad have already been dealt with in the chapter on fish; it may be added that no Cape cook would have dreamed of making a crayfish salad from the tail flesh alone; the indispensable parts were supposed to be the soft flesh immediately under the carapace, the meat from the claws, and the green "mush" that is found near the coral.

Before we finish with sauce, it is desirable to say something about a sauce that is rarely used by itself but is indispensable for the making of many dishes. This is *kerrie sous* or *curry sauce*, in whose preparation the Malay cook demonstrated the highest skill of his craft. It was essentially a braise of many different spices, with herbs, vegetables, salt and sugar, in butter or fat, to which was added, as a thinning, tamarind water or vinegar and coconut milk. The most elaborate recipe is also one of the oldest, and although half of the ingredients mentioned in it may be omitted, it is here given as a curiosity to show how the old cooks proceeded when they had no means

sauces of obtaining ready-made curry powder.

To make a good curry sauce. Pound separately in your mortar (which you must wipe out after each pounding with a little coconut milk) green ginger, fennel seed, aniseed, allspice, coriander seed, cardamon seed, a peach kernel and three blanched almonds, green and red chillies, mace, nutmeg, black pepper, cloves and fresh lemon peel. Cut up very finely an onion and a few cloves of garlic, with some thyme, basil, celery, sage and rosemary, and braise them in a little sheep's fat. When brown, add a few cumin seeds. Take all that you have pounded and mix it intimately with powdered turmeric, till it has a fine yellow colour; moisten it with tamarind water and stir it into the braised onion and garlic; add more tamarind water to make a thick sauce. This you can use for making any curry, by frying your meat in it. If you think it burns the tongue too much, you may mellow it by adding sugar or by reducing the amount of chillies.

Sometimes such a curry sauce, made in a far less elaborate fashion, was prepared for home use and stored in a bottle or jar. Very soon (it seems as early as 1670) a curry powder composed of all the necessary ingredients was imported from China. A convicted Chinaman, who was sent out as a prisoner to the Cape, is said to have first used it. Tradition also has it that he was the first to keep a restaurant, somewhere on the shore of Rogge Bay, which was where the war monument now stands. Later, so tradition avers, he was sent for on occasion to the Castle to cook special dinners for Governor Simon van der Stel who was a gentleman of good taste and liked to eat a well-cooked dish.

From the beginning of the eighteenth century, curry powder was invariably employed in making curry sauce; in my young days I knew of only one cook who still made the old-fashioned and almost obsolete curry paste — the old artist who ruled the kitchen (and menagerie in the back yard) at the White House Hotel in Strand Street, then the recognised Mecca of all who wished to taste good Malay cookery.

The *sambals* were Oriental relishes that were highly popular at the Cape, but somehow do not appear to have appealed to English taste. Miss Morris, who edited Mrs Rundle's cookery book, and who had visited the Cape where she doubtless copied the recipe for her *"Ragout of Lambstones"*, does not mention them; neither does Mrs Kindersley who came later. According to the Coloured butler who, many years later when "Major Wellesley" had reached fame, gave his recollection of the Duke of Wellington, the Duke liked "quince sambal" and asked for it whenever he came to dine at the hospitable Newlands house of the richest man in the Colony.

Sambals are in theory very easy to make; they are simply finely chopped fresh fruit or vegetables, dressed with simple spices or herbs and a little vinegar or lemon juice. In practice, however, a great deal of skill is necessary

98

to serve them smooth, fresh and virgin in their colouring, **sauces**
for within a couple of hours they lose their crispness and
turn brown. They must therefore be made immediately
before they are to be used and the several kinds, each in
its own little glass dish, are presented on a salver from
which the guest may help himself to a few spoonfuls at a
time. They are served as a rule with all curries, sometimes
with meat or fish dishes. The favourites are:

Apple sambal. Peel and grate a sour apple and half a
sweet one; mix with a little salt, red pepper, grated nutmeg
and lemon juice.

Quince sambal. Peel and grate a ripe quince; if it is a
borrie or turmeric quince, the sambal will be a pale yellow
colour; ordinary quince sambal, like apple sambal, should
be snowy white. Mix the grated flesh with lemon juice,
powdered chilli and white pepper and a little salt.

Cucumber sambal. Take a young cucumber, peel it and
remove the seeds; mince it finely, and strew salt on it; let it
stand for a quarter of an hour; pour off the water that has
drained from it, and lightly dry the mince in a thin cloth.
Mix well with a little vinegar, white pepper and lemon
juice.

Apricot sambal. Peel and seed firm, not quite ripe,
apricots, and chop them fine; mix with a little lemon juice,
salt, and white pepper.

Onion sambal. Scald a large white onion and chop it up;
mix with salt, pepper, a pinch of chillies, some chopped
marjoram and a little vinegar.

Radish sambal. Clean and grate raw unpeeled radish;
mix with red pepper, salt, a little minced onion and some
vinegar.

Banana sambal. Pare a firm, not too ripe, banana and
chop it into small dice; mix with red pepper, salt, minced
marjoram and a little lemon juice.

Carrot sambal. Grate young raw carrots; mix with salt,
grated nutmeg, very little white pepper and vinegar or
lemon juice.

Mixed herbs sambal. Chop up finely marjoram, fennel,
thyme, mint, parsley, scented verbena, celery and young
sorrel leaves with a green chilli; mix them to a paste with a
little tamarind water, salt and sugar.

Loquat and spring onion sambal. Take large ripe loquats;
plunge them into boiling water and peel them; take out,
seed and dry. Chop them into very small pieces, with some
spring onions, a pinch of red pepper, ginger and salt; mix
intimately with lemon juice in which a little vinegar has
been stirred.

sauces   Any vegetable or fruit that is capable of being grated or minced without losing its crispness is suitable for a sambal. It is this "crunchiness" that, combined with the sharp pungency of the chillies, gives the sambal its appetising taste and that makes it so valuable as a relish for a hot curry.

Salad materials are plentiful in South Africa, but the old cooks favoured for their vegetable salads lettuce and cabbage. Both were usually, and unfortunately, shredded, mixed with a boiled beetroot, raw onions and a dressing either of simple vinegar, salt and pepper, or vinegar in which these condiments were beaten up with egg yolk and an oil in the form of melted butter or the clarified oil obtained from sheep's trotters.

The garnishing was hard-boiled eggs cut in slices, as for the meat and fish salads.

With the exception of salads made from certain indigenous plants, all the recipes follow the ordinary rules of the European cook books and it is unnecessary to give any examples. Fruit salads, in which some modifications were introduced, will be dealt with in a later chapter.

Chapter IX

VEGETABLES

THE settlers started by planting vegetables from seeds brought with them from Holland. These flourished exceedingly well as Van Riebeeck, an enthusiastic gardener, noted in his Log. For several years the Settlement was supplied with vegetables from the Company's garden; then from the farm in the neighbourhood of Green Point Common. But when the Free Burghers were granted allotments, vegetables were extensively grown and were sold in what became the first general market. Since then vegetables, including all the varieties known to European cooks, were easily procurable. There is no reason why vegetable foodstuffs should ever be scarce in the country, for it has excellent garden soil and all that is wanted is intensive cultivation and an absence of bureaucratic control.

Early Cape cooks followed the Continental method of preparing vegetables for the table, with the result that cooked vegetables retained their flavour and sometimes much of their succulence. They were never plainly boiled in water; soda was never used in cooking them; they were discarded if not fresh and untainted; and when they were combined with other foodstuffs care was taken not to destroy their individual taste. The cooking of vegetables at the Cape was favourably commented on by several writers. While epicures like Baron von Boechenroeder, an "Indian Officer", complained that meat dishes in the Colony were always greasy and sometimes overstewed — neither of which accusations is substantiated by the

vege- recipes – they agreed that so far as the vegetable cookery
tables was concerned "It compared favourably with the best
Italian."

That was deserved praise.

English cooks, as Wharton and others have testified,
have always ill-treated their vegetables ; even today, when
they have learned a great deal, they seem to be more concerned about retaining the vitamins, that are of no
importance whatever in a properly mixed diet, than about
preserving the original individuality of the vegetable or
felicitously improving its palatability by blending it with
an alien spicy or aromatic flavour.

Such old manuscript cookery books as give what may
be regarded as general hints for the cook state that
vegetables preferably must be steamed ; at any rate they
should all be cooked very slowly, especially when they
are past their prime. For some young vegetables the Malay
cooks recommended a quick, short immersion in boiling
water ; all are agreed that plain boiled vegetable is not a
dish to set before anyone. The directives for "finishing"
a vegetable are thus many and varied and it is interesting
to see how closely they follow the recipes contained in
Dutch, Flemish, German and Italian cookery books of the
seventeenth century. They speak of "dry-cooking" (*droog-
kook*) which really is sauteeing in butter or fat, with the
difference that the vegetable is not allowed, as in a true
sautee, to become slightly impregnated with the oil ; of
mashing or making a puree of the vegetable ; of creaming,
which means slow simmering in cream ; and of glazing,
in which the vegetable was stewed in a jelly-bouillon
with a little butter and sugar. They hardly ever prepared a
true *frittura*, in which the vegetable was plunged into
boiling oil or fat ; a frying basket rarely figured among their
kitchen utensils, for they preferred to deal with their vegetables by shallow-frying or by frying in batter.

Great care was taken in cleaning the vegetables, and
usually the first paragraphs of the recipes are devoted to
instructions how this should be done. These are omitted,
and in the examples here given it is presupposed that the
ingredients have been properly shorn of whatever is
extraneous.

We may now describe some of the ways in which the
various vegetables were dealt with, referring the reader
who wishes to know about the preparation of indigenous
vegetables to the later chapter on Veld Food. Only such
recipes as exhibit some modification that may reasonably
be regarded as of local invention are given.

Potatoes: A popular method was to steam them in their
skins, with a little salt, thyme leaves and green ginger in
the pot, and to send them to table with melted butter
served in a sauce boat. For made-dishes, they were
treated like this, the skins drawn off, and the potatoes
used as directed. Otherwise they were thinly peeled before being cooked. Fried, boiled, buttered, roast, sauteed
and baked potatoes were made exactly in accordance with
European recipes ; the only difference is that peeled
boiled potatoes were never sent to the table without first

being "tossed" in a little butter and having nutmeg grated over them.

Herbs were most frequently used in flavouring them; when spice was used it was generally nutmeg, pepper or allspice, chillies being considered incompatible except in a potatoe bredie. Mashed potatoes were creamed by adding butter, cream and egg yolk and a seasoning of nutmeg.

Potatoes with wine. Beat up two large boiled mealy potatoes with some grated nutmeg, an ounce of salt butter and a glass of sherry; add the yolks of two eggs. Shape it into a loaf; paint it with egg yolk beaten up with a little of the white, dust it with breadcrumbs and bake it in a buttered dish in the oven. When it is golden brown all over, drench it with a sauce made of egg yolk, wine, sugar and nutmeg, with a little salt, that you have allowed to simmer till moderately thick. Serve at once with any meat dish.

Hot potato snow. Steam large, mealy potatoes in their skins with a little ginger, herbs and a bit of lemon rind. Peel them and press them through a sieve, so that the flakes fall lightly on the dish. Dust with powdered nutmeg and salt and a little pepper mixed, and serve as hot as possible.

Potato rice. Make a rather stiff potato puree and press it through a colander on a hot dish, holding the colander some distance above the dish, so that the little balls of potato form a pyramid. Dust with pepper and salt, place in a quick oven for a few minutes and serve.

Potato dumplings. Make a puree with some mealy potatoes, butter, salt, pepper, grated nutmeg and egg yolk; thicken if necessary with a little rice flour; form into small round balls and boil in bouillon. A variation of this directs that the whites of eggs should be stiffly whipped and incorporated in the dumpling mixture, which must then be scooped up in a spoon which is dipped into the boiling soup or bouillon; this is certainly an easier method to make the dumplings which have an unfortunate propensity to disintegrate.

Potatoes with tail fat. Put peeled potatoes in a flat pot with sufficient sheep's tail fat to cover the bottom; strew salt and a little marjoram over the potatoes. Put on the lid and let the potatoes stew till they are well done, shaking the pot occasionally. Another, and better way is:

Braise diced pork fat with some chopped parsley, a bay leaf, salt, pepper and nutmeg; stir in a cup of strong broth or bouillon and put in your potatoes, which must be already boiled and mealy. Put on the lid and allow to stew slowly for 20 minutes.

Potato curry. Cut boiled potatoes in slices and stew these lightly in a sharp curry sauce, taking care that they are not broken.

Vinegar potatoes. Melt two ounces of butter in a pan and
mix it smoothly with one ounce sifted flour; when it
begins to get brown, stir into it a tablespoonful of vinegar,
a tablespoonful of brown sugar, pepper and salt and a
cupful of broth (or wine). Boil it till it has the consistency
of cream, and slice into it four large peeled potatoes. Let it
simmer gently till the potatoes are quite tender and serve
with some minced onion strewn over.

Potato cheese. Boil four pounds of potatoes in their
skins with onions, ginger, salt and pepper; peel them, and
mash them well; put the mash in a jar with a pound's weight
of new milk and a teaspoonful of rennet, a teaspoonful of
caraway and aniseed mixed, and a few coriander seeds;
knead the mixture well, and put it aside, covered with a
damp cloth, in a cool place for four or five days; knead it
again, press out all moisture, and put the mixture in a
mould, and let it stand till it begins to show cracks on its
surface; paint these over with a mixture of sour milk and
cream. When the cheese is hard on its outside, which will
be in about a month's time, you may use it like any
ordinary cheese.

One recipe advised that the cheese should be coloured
with saffron. It is by no means bad eating and is comparatively easy to make.

Asparagus: There are several indigenous varieties,
though the cultivated kind has been a favourite from
very early days. Up to the end of the past century, one
could buy large bunches of the local "wild" asparagus
from the hawkers in Cape Town streets, generally at a
penny a bunch. It was then a very cheap vegetable, although it was regarded as a delicacy of which Rhodes
was known to be very fond. The local product was thin,
long, very green and exquisitely flavoured; nowadays it
is almost impossible to get, and the thick, often woody,
etiolated cultivated fronds have taken its place. It was
always steamed, with a little salt, and served with melted
butter, its flavour being regarded as too delicate to be
benefited by any spice or herb. It was also used for
soups, and a puree of the boiled plant was sometimes
sophisticated with spices and breadcrumbs and baked in
the oven.

Mushrooms were never popular, and there are few
recipes that are not copied from Dutch or English books
for their preparation, although many varieties of edible
mushrooms are to be found on the veld. So far as my
investigations go, there is no special South African modification for preparing them, and all recipes that mention
them, as constituents of dishes, are merely copies of already published directives.

Endive was stewed, made into a bredie, or served as a
puree, always with nutmeg, pepper, plenty of butter and
sometimes with a meat gravy. *Lettuce* was similarly
treated, and both vegetables were, like *spinach*, thought
to have considerable tonic value.

Aubergine or *egg-plant*, of which there are several

varieties, was known as *brinjal*. It was excellently served by itself, stewed, braised, sauteed and even grilled, or in combination with other vegetables and meats. It was also stuffed with one of the farces mentioned in a former chapter, or served with poached eggs. A curious recipe is the following, which produces, as I can testify from personal experience, a most tasty dish:

Aubergine with pine kernels. Select your brinjals with care, choosing a moderate-sized one, with firm and thick flesh; peel it thinly and cut it in slices, on which you strew salt; let the brinjal lie till most of the water has been extracted; then wipe the slices and dust them with fine flour which you have previously mixed with powdered white pepper, ginger and nutmeg; slice and brown some onions with fat; lay on them the brinjal slices and strew over them plenty of pine kernels; then add enough sherry to cover them and stew with the lid closed, till everything is well blended. A little chilli and a teaspoonful of *blatjang* added much improves it.

Artichoke: Both kinds, the girasole or Jerusalem and the globe variety, are mentioned in the recipes, but neither has interested the Cape cook sufficiently to stimulate his inventive ingenuity, although the former is responsible for the following two recipes:

Banana artichokes. Dice some artichokes that have been steamed in wine; put the pieces of artichoke in a saucepan, slice on them the bananas; add a lump of butter, a little salt, pepper and parsley; let them simmer for a few minutes; add a glass of sherry, and a little flour to thicken; shake well and add some more salt if required, and finally a cup of boiling thin cream. Serve with nutmeg grated over.

Artichokes with penguin eggs. Puree cooked artichokes and mix it with the mashed yolks of hard boiled penguin eggs. Add salt, pepper, a little powdered chilli, a blade of mace, a glass of sherry; let it simmer on the fire, stirring constantly, till it no longer cleaves to the side of the saucepan. Take out and serve on a dish with the jellied white of the eggs as a decoration.

Beetroot: One of the oldest recipes is also one of the best, even though it has no other title than:

How to prepare beetroot. A dozen young beetroots, none larger than a bantam's egg; two large, flat white onions; six shallots; a tablespoonful of honey; a tablespoonful of sifted wheat flour; leaves of the herb marjoram; two tablespoonsful fat; a teaspoonful of vinegar; as much salt as will savour. Scrape the beets and cut them into quarters; smother (braise) the onions and shallots, herb and salt in the fat, add the beets and let them slowly simmer till they are soft, which will take only a few minutes. Add the flour, honey and vinegar, beaten up, and let it all stew for half an hour, when you can serve it with rice.

vege- This was obviously a bourgeois recipe; it is much
tables improved by adding spices, substituting sugar for honey
and tamarind water for the vinegar. But even without these
improvements, it makes a very nice dish, either hot or
cold.

Beans: There are so many varieties of beans that few,
outside the bureaucrats of an Agricultural Department, can
classify them. For the cook, however, they may all be
lumped into two simple categories – green beans and
dried beans. Both were standard foodstuffs at the Cape
from the earliest times. From the East came those magnificent dried beans that were known as *katjang boontjies*
and many others, some as small as a peppercorn, others
nearly an inch and a half oval. The method of preparing
them was invariably the same. Soak your beans overnight
in cold water, rejecting those that float; stew them gently
in fat, with a glass of wine as zest, and season them with
braised onions, herbs, spices and chillies.

You ate them hot with their own sauce, or cold with a
sour sauce. You made them into bredie with some pieces
of fat neck, or rib of lamb or mutton. You dealt similarly
with dried peas and broad beans. A "Recipe for the less
affluent", as the old cook books quaintly put it, dictated
a slow cooking, in an earthenware jar – possibly one of
the smaller jars that contained sesame oil from Tonkin –
in an oven, with bits of bacon, onions, chillies, ginger and
garden herbs. A simple sort of baked beans, but for all
that much superior to the canned variety we now get.
Much later, tomatoes were incorporated with the beans,
and there are recipes that insist on butter and many
spices that were only within the means of the rich.

Green beans were used when young and tender, and
the best kind was always a butter bean, pale yellow in
colour. It was steamed in wine and butter, with some
herbs; or in a very little broth, and served with a covering
of a sour sauce and a dusting of grated nutmeg. Cold, it
was equally tasty with such a sauce. A green bean bredie
was a dish by itself, rich, savoury and filling. Sometimes
little pieces of quince were added to it and, more rarely, a
chunk or two of potato.

Green peas were treated in the same manner. Some
kinds could be eaten, when cooked, with the pods, but
commonly the beans were shelled, very gently steamed
with butter and a little water with a snippet of onion, a
leaf of marjoram and a teaspoonful of honey and served
with a dusting of nutmeg. Mint was not supposed to be
the best flavouring to blend with them and, indeed, mint
does overpower the delicacy of their juvenile savour.

Indian peas or groundnuts, were never eaten when fresh,
but, when dried, were made into purees; sometimes they
were first roasted, pounded in a mortar with chillies and
breadcrumbs, salt and pepper, made into patties and
fried in fat, but they were never popular, and their taste is
not to everyone's liking.

Cabbage, Brussels sprouts, and *red cabbage* were all
much liked and there are many recipes for their preparation. Again, as these vegetables were old friends from the

homelands, they were dealt with in accordance with vege- European methods of serving and cooking. The only tables difference was that they were never overcooked, always sent to table with some butter and a grating of nutmeg on them, and steamed or stewed rather than plain boiled.

Cauliflower, spinach, celery, carrots, onions, leeks, shallots, parsnips and *turnips* could be cooked in much the same fashion and though, for them too, there are all sorts of recipes, the same qualification applied. Nearly all

of them make good bredie, and all can be steamed or braised in accordance with the directions already given; flavouring is a matter of taste and discretion.

Gourd vegetables, of which the various *squashes, cucumbers* and *pumpkins* are the main representatives, were sometimes cooked a little differently, as the following recipes show:

Fried squashes. Peel them and slice thin; dust the slices with pepper, a little turmeric and salt; roll them in fine flour and fry them quickly in a shallow pan with plenty of fat; drain, pile on a dish, strew fine breadcrums over and serve them at once. It would be better to deep-fry them in a basket, as the Italians do, but the real *frittura* was almost unknown in South Africa.

Cucumbers with cream. Steam young cucumbers with a little white wine, herbs and salt; remove their seeds, and cut them up into square pieces; put in a shallow dish, with butter, pepper, salt, nutmeg and a cupful of thick cream; let simmer, shaking often. Serve with a dusting of dried parsley.

Boiled squash. Put the whole squash in a saucepan with a little water, salt and herbs. Steam till soft. Serve whole or cut into two parts, with melted butter.

This is the usual way of serving the small green, rounded squash known as *marakka*. If young enough its seeds are soft and entirely eatable, but older specimens must have the seeds scooped out before they are sent to table.

107

Pumpkin, cucumber or squash fritters. **These are made
with a puree of the cooked vegetable, spiced with cinnamon, mace, honey (or sugar nowadays), ginger and a little
salt. A little rice flour or sifted meal is sometimes added to
make a firmer dough, which is shaped into flat patties or
cakes and fried in fat or butter, and served with a mixture of
sugar and cinnamon, either as dessert or as an accompaniment of a bobotie or curry.**

All gourd vegetables may be used for bredies, but as
they contain much water, the stew pot should be left open
to allow for evaporation and the cooking should be prolonged and very slow, great care being taken to prevent
burning. Even at their best, such gourd bredies are not
equal to those made from other vegetables, and their
goodness depends much on what is added to them by
way of spices and herbs.

Mielies, or *Indian corn* came into the Settlement in the
early part of the eighteenth century when the Company
urged every householder to plant maize to augment the
food supply for the slaves, as it was difficult to import
sufficient quantities of rice.

Since then it has always been a favourite as a green
vegetable, on the farms, but it has never really come
into its own in the towns. Even now hotel cooks do not
seem to know how to serve it properly and usually spoil
it in the cooking. Sugar corn is grown extensively for the
market, but the best eating mielie is still the old fashioned
bread mielie which has a far larger grain and when
eaten young is unsurpassed by any of the newer kinds.
And let it be said that an old mielie, whose grain has already hardened, is quite unfit for the table; no manner of
cooking it can make it worth while to eat it, for it is
tasteless, without flavour, and not easily digested. So
choose young, fresh mielies, whose grain is tender, and
whose "beard" or stigmas, are still transparently green,
and treat them in accordance with one of the following
recipes:

Boiled mielies. **Divest the cobs of their outer leaves, but
let the last, almost translucent inner layer abide; take
away also the "beard"; plunge them into boiling water, to
which you have added some salt, and let them boil
rapidly until the grains are soft. Take out and drain, and
serve on a flat dish, handing round melted butter with
them.**

A few hints in connection with this; do not send them
to table with butter on them; serve the butter separately;
some people much prefer to butter them with unmelted
butter; send them piping hot. The proper way to eat them
is to butter them, grasp the ends of the cob with the
hands protected by a napkin, and bite off the grain.

The guest who has a rocking denture is advised to cut
the grain from the cob and eat it with a spoon or a fork.

Baked mielies. **Put the whole mielie, still covered with**

108

a layer of leaf, on the hot ash of a wood fire and rake over it more ash and some glowing embers. Turn it frequently; it generally takes from ten to 20 minutes to bake properly; strip off the burnt leaves, and serve as with boiled mielies.

They can also be baked in the oven or grilled on a gridiron in this way.

Fried green mielies. Cut the grain from the young cobs, sprinkle with salt and pepper, and fry in fat till they are a golden brown; drain, heap on a dish, sprinkle with dried parsley and serve.

Mielie bread (Indian corn pudding). Cut the grain from a dozen cooked cobs and pound it in a mortar; mix it with two beaten eggs, pepper, salt, a blade of mace, some grated nutmeg, a cup of milk and a cup of cream. Fill a greased mould with this mixture and steam for half an hour. Take out, cut into slices and serve with melted butter, or a sour sauce.

This is an excellent, delicious-tasting vegetable pudding which is usually served as an accompaniment to roast meat, particularly pork. It is not easy to make in perfection, but any care taken in its preparation is well repaid by the result.

A sweet dish is made from dried mielies, the recipe for which will be given later. From the cooked grain of fresh green mielies a number of made dishes can be prepared by mixing them with various other ingredients. A *mielie bredie* is not often met with, but is quite good. Another mixed dish is to stew the grain with braised onions and tomatoes; or mix it with eggs beaten up and fry the mixture to the consistency of buttered eggs.

Many other combinations will suggest themselves to the ingenious cook. One such is to steam the young mielies, entirely denuded of their covering leaves, in a little white wine, with herbs and spices; the result is something different from the ordinary "boiled green mielies" and well worth trying.

Purslane (*porseleinblaar*) that grows profusely in every Cape garden in late winter and spring was, in the old days, and should be today, a favourite vegetable. Its little succulent leaves were gathered, washed and braised with ginger powder, mace, pepper and salt in fat; a tiny spicule of garlic was added, a wineglassful of wine was stirred in, and the result was an amazingly delicate, luscious and sapid puree, that was served with rice and potatoes.

Okra was introduced about the same time as tomatoes and the usual way to serve it was in the Creole fashion. The downy outer covering was scrapped off, the pods were thrown into vinegar and water, dried, and then steamed or boiled in water till soft. Then they were drained and braised in casserole with butter, chillies, a little sugar and salt to taste, and served on or with fried bread.

109

Sometimes tiny bits of pineapple were incorporated in the braise, which was glutinous rather than succulent.

Sweet potatoes: Three principal kinds were on the market, and all three are still obtainable. The best are the large-sized tubers that "cut white"; they must be firm and old, woody tubers should never be used. They can be used just like potatoes; a favourite method is to bake them in their skins under the ashes or in the oven. In this form they are the chief food of the poor in country districts. A better way is to stew them.

Gestoofde patats (stewed sweet potatoes). Peel and cut into slices four young, moderately sized tubers; put them in salted water, then take them out and dry them carefully. Place in an iron pot, with a large lump of sheep's tail fat or butter, a cupful of honey (or sugar) some sifted flour, a feather of cinnamon, a blade of mace, and some salt; pour over a cup of boiling water; let it all simmer very slowly, shaking the pot but not stirring the contents which remain whole.

Stewed sweet potatoes should be translucent, golden with a slightly brownish tinge (topaz-tinted in fact) and exquisitely tender. They are served as a sweet vegetable with roast meat and roast chicken, and hardly ever as a dessert dish.

Rice: This cereal was indisputably the chief vegetable in the old Cape household, and is today still regarded as absolutely indispensable at every well-cooked dinner. The correct way of preparing it was the Indian way, which produced two kinds of boiled rice, one known as "dry rice" (*droë rys*) and the other as "wet rice" (*pap rys*). The rice was cleaned (not necessarily always washed, although some cooks rinsed it in several waters till the liquid remained clear; others held that this removed a great deal of the goodness from the grains) and thrown into rapidly-boiling water. A little salt was added and the boiling was continued till the grains were soft; the rice was then strained on a colander, which was allowed to remain on top of the pot so that the steam from the water in which the rice had been boiled could rise up and percolate through it. In this way the rice grains swelled and lost enough of their outer moistness, while retaining all their inside sapidity, to become "dry rice", where each grain was separate, distinct and entirely loose from the other.

If wet rice was desired, the grains were not strained off but were allowed to simmer slowly in the original water till they had absorbed almost all the liquid; the result was a pasty mass, in which each grain adhered to its fellows without, however, having lost its individuality and still retaining its shape.

Wet rice was preferred for some dishes; dry rice for others. It was regarded as distinctly bad taste to serve one kind with a dish that tradition prescribed should be accompanied by the other kind.

Rice was always served as a vegetable; a rice pudding was quite unknown, and the first recipe for it appears late

and is obviously taken from a European cookery book —
although it has been much modified so that, if its directions
are followed, what comes out is not the ordinary insipid
and gruel-like sweet of the nursery, but a glorified sweet
pilaf of preserved peel, raisins, dates and nuts, cooked in
plenty of butter and a rich custard cream.

Rice was also rarely made into sophisticated dishes,
though it was much used for soups and was sometimes
made into a bredie. The recipes for chicken, ham, mutton
and fish pilafs do not greatly differ from those that were
familiar to Occidental cooks, except that they all prescribe a variety of spices and prolonged cooking; nearly
every one can be paralleled by some particular Italian
risotto. The most popular of these combined dishes is:

Yellow rice (geel rys). Take dry boiled rice; put it in a
saucepan with butter, turmeric powder, a small piece of
green ginger, a tablespoonful of moist brown sugar, a
teaspoonful of salt and a little powdered chilli; add a
cupful of stoned raisins; moisten with bouillon, and allow
to simmer. One old recipe substitutes saffron for the
turmeric powder. The rice should be "wet" when dished
up, with all the ingredients well mixed, and it should not
be too sweet.

Two other combined rice recipes are:

Quince rice. Mix dry, boiled rice with grated green
quinces and some pounded cheese, pepper, salt and a little
powdered chilli; put in a greased pie dish; add a little
onion juice mixed in a glass of sherry; steam, and serve
with a meat sauce.

Rice with penguin eggs. Make a strong meat gravy;
mix with a glass of sherry and beat into it a teaspoonful
of sour fruit jelly (kei-apple jelly). Let it boil up and pour
through a sieve. Put a layer of dry boiled rice in a pie dish,
and place on it two hardboiled penguin eggs cut into
quarters or slices; fill up with rice; pour over the sauce,
bake for a few minutes in the oven, and serve.

Tomatoes were a comparatively late introduction, but
when the Malay cooks realised how useful they can be
they did not hesitate to make bredie of them or to use
them for mixed dishes. Their wateriness needs to be
counteracted by prolonged slow steaming with the lid off
the pot, to allow for evaporation. Most of the recipes for
their preparation are, with the exception of the bredie, not
original but copies from printed directives that have been
adapted to local taste.

Thus *tamatie blatjang* (tomato chutney-sauce) is
merely a variant of tomato puree to which various spices
have been added with a fruit puree. A good tomato bredie
made with fat mutton, spices, herbs and a glass of wine,
should be neither watery nor greasy; it needs at least
three hours slow, steady simmering. But when well made
it is one of the outstanding *bredies* and should be served
with white "dry" rice, boiled, buttered and nutmegged
potatoes and a sweet chutney.

111

Chapter X

VELDKOS OR FOOD FROM THE VELD

VELDKOS may be interpreted in two senses, either as "food produced by or derived from the veld" or "food to be eaten on the veld", veld being any uncultivated part of the countryside. In practice only the first interpretation is assigned to the word. In this chapter *veldkos* means edible uncultivated wild foodstuffs that are made eatable according to the old Cape recipes.

The earliest travellers relate how wonderfully prolific in "herbs and plants" were the flat lands round Table Bay in winter and spring after the early rains. Jacquin, the famous gardener of Schönbrun, writing about a Cape sorrel, noted: *Illam se invenisse anno 1653 in promontorio bonae spei ad pedem montis leonum, ubi magna copia colligebatur et ad naves deferebatur ut cum aliis herbis in olus coqueretur.* Before that date, however, ships sailing round the Cape had landed sailors to collect baskets of sorrel which, made into a stew, was regarded as a prophylactic against and a cure for scurvy.

Jan van Riebeeck found fine examples of wild asparagus, "as good as anything in the homeland", growing on the slopes of Table Mountain. From his time onwards travellers have mentioned various wild plants that were used as foodstuffs by both colonists and Africans.

Some of them are so rare, so local and little-known that they must be regarded as curiosities with which only a few cooks are acquainted. Others were, and to some extent still are, popular and comparatively easy to procure. The following kinds could all be had in season on the Cape Town market at the end of the past century, when dishes made from them could be readily obtained at one or other of the hotels or boarding houses that specialised in Cape dishes. Today most of them would have to be **veldkos** procured through the intervention of some kindly farmer friend although, as a matter of fact, some of them are to be found within walking distance of Cape Town.

Wateruintjies: The flowers and flower pods of the water hawthorn (*aponogeton diastychon*) that blooms on waterpools from April to September.

Sanduintjies: The corms of a blue-white Iris (*morea edule*) in season in August-October.

Geeluintjies: The corms of a yellow-flowered variety of the same species, reputed to be more delicate in flavour.

Bobbejaanuintjies: The bulbs of *oxalis lupinifolia jacq* or the corms of species of *babiana* and *cyanella*, season in winter and spring.

Sorrel: The leaves of the wild sorrel (*oxalis pes caprae*), in season from August to October.

Veldkool (wild cabbage). The flower buds of a species of *anthericum*, often growing as high as five feet, and in season in April and May.

Jakkalskos (fox food) : The fruit of a parasite, *hydnora africana*, in season in the early summer.

Baroe and kameroe: The large underground tubers of plants that grow in sandy and clay soil, usually *syphias*, in season in September to December.

Wild fennel and *wild anise:* The fleshy rootstocks of various plants belonging to the carrot family, in season in summer.

Ghoo: The seeds of the wild almond tree (*brabejum stellatifolium*).

In addition, there are many kinds of wild berries and fruits and at least one kind of *aloe* that are edible, and whose names figure in old recipes. As most of them are unobtainable on the market, nothing more need be said about them.

Water hawthorn (*wateruintjies*)*:* This is undoubtedly the most popular of all the edible wild plants, and anyone who travels by road through the country will notice its beautiful white, strongly-scented flowers studding the surface of quiet wayside pools almost hiding the small, lancet shaped leaves. It has a thick, fleshy bulb which is edible, but is rarely used, the flower buds being much preferred. Bundles of these can still be bought on the Cape Town Parade and sometimes in the streets from itinerant hawkers, four bunches making a *kooksel*, or sufficient for an average dish. The flowers must be fresh, partly-opened, with the calyces bright green; if the buds are old and mahogany coloured, they should be rejected. They will keep fairly well in a cool place for a couple of days. They are prepared as follows:

Stewed. Wash the buds and remove the stalks; put them in a stewpot with a lump of fat or butter, salt, pepper, a little chopped onion, a few thyme leaves and a bay leaf; let them simmer gently, then add a handful of chopped sorrel leaves, and allow to simmer for a little while longer; stir in a glass of sherry and serve.

veldkos   Some cooks always prefer to parboil the buds in a little salt water, throwing away the wine-coloured liquid, but this is not necessary.

Bredie. Braise good fat neck or rib of mutton, cut into suitable pieces, in a pot with some onion slices, a pinch of powdered ginger, a crushed chilli, a blade of mace and some salt and pepper. As soon as the meat is nicely browned, put in the buds, with a handful of sorrel leaves finely minced; let it simmer for a couple of hours, adding a tablespoonful of wine from time to time, and stirring well. Finally stir in a tablespoonful of a good chutney sauce, and dish up with boiled rice.

With coriander. Proceed as before, omitting the spices; stir in a teaspoonful of crushed coriander seed; finish by stirring in a cupful of boiling cream.

With eggs. Make a puree of stewed buds, and mix it with cream, a pinch of tangerine peel pounded fine, and a teaspoonful of China (soya) sauce; fill small ramikin dishes with the puree, and place on each a newlaid egg; place in the oven till the egg is lightly set; powder with grated nutmeg and serve.

Soufflé. Make a puree of stewed buds and beat it till it is very fine. For each pound of the puree take four eggs; mix the yolks of these in the puree; beat the whites to a stiff froth, and fold in the mixture; bake in a quick oven and serve at once.

One recipe mixes chopped anchovies with the puree.

Baked. Mix a puree of stewed buds with boiled, mealy potatoes, well mashed with some butter and cream; form into cakes or balls and fry in butter or fat. Sprinkle with salt and pepper and serve.

With bananas. Peel and fry the bananas in boiling fat; put them round the sides of a deep pie dish, and fill the dish with a puree of the buds; pour over a couple of egg yolks beaten up in a cup of milk and bake in the oven.

With fish. This is simply any kind of steamed fish served on a bed of the puree and covered with either a sour or a fish sauce. It was usually garnished with peeled hanepoot grapes which had been preserved in brandy, and made an attractive, interesting dish.

As soup. The puree was stirred into a good chicken soup, to which a dash of cream was added; it was served with croutons of fried bread.

Tomatoes and potatoes were sometimes filled with the puree and either stewed or baked in the oven. The puree was also used as a filling for tartlets, as a basis for patties, and as a cold sambal. Instead of the usual admixture of

114

·sorrel leaves, which were intended to give a tinge of **veldkos** acidity to the dish, lemon juice or tamarind water was often used.

Wild cabbage was dealt with in much the same way, but as it has a less pronounced flavour, it was considered bad cookery to add chillies or too much pepper to it. It needed no preliminary parboiling, and was best prepared as a stew by itself, or as a bredie with meat and very little onion. Many epicures prefer it to *wateruintjies* and as a matter of fact its flavour is more delicate than that of any wild plant; while a creamed puree made from it far surpasses that made from spinach, broad bean or turnip tops. All that is required is to simmer it gently with wine,

butter, mace and a little salt and pepper; mash it thoroughly when tender, and mix it with cream; then it is replaced on the stove, and allowed to heat quietly, without boiling, and served with dry white rice and boiled potatoes.

It is indeed so excellent that one wonders why no enterprising nurseryman has deemed it worth his while to cultivate the plant and introduce it to the general public as a garden vegetable. In season it grows abundantly on all the hill slopes in certain parts and can be gathered without difficulty, yet one never sees it exposed for sale on the streets and few, outside the country towns, know of its existence.

The bulb *uintjies* need different methods of preparation. In the first place, their collection in the field demands an exact knowledge of the different kinds of iris, for some species have bulbs that are not only not edible but poisonous, and there are some cases on record where children eating them have died. The native collectors, however, are fully aware of the distinctions between the different varieties, and their harvest may be trusted. Although there are several kinds, all the edible *uintjies* are cherry-sized and shaped bulbs, almond white inside, and covered outside by a fibrous husk which is easily pulled off. They taste somewhat like chestnuts and, when boiled have the same crisp consistency, can be mashed easily and blend perfectly with many flavourings. They may be baked under the ashes or in the oven, boiled like ordinary chestnuts, or made into a puree from which different dishes can be prepared.

Normally the bunch of bulbs, tied together by one of the rushlike leaves of the plant itself, is boiled in a little

veldkos salt water, and served on a dish, each guest helping himself to a few of the bulbs, peeling off the husk, and eating the bulb with a little salt and pepper or melted butter. They are prepared more elaborately as follows:

Soup. The recipe for this has been given already, in the chapter on Soups.

Creamed. The boiled bulbs are mashed to a fine puree which is passed through a sieve, mixed with grated nutmeg, salt, a little melted butter and boiling cream.

Pudding. A creamed puree is made in accordance with the directions in the previous paragraph, and is mixed with honey (or sugar) and yolk of egg. The whites of the eggs are whipped to a stiff froth and incorporated in the mixture, which is steamed in a buttered mould. The pudding is served with a sweet sauce when it is used as a dessert dish, and with a sour sauce when it is dished up as an accompaniment to a roast. It is delightfully bland. As a sweet dish the addition of a few pounded bitter almonds improves it.

Wild sorrel, of which the stalks as well as the leaves are used, is added to bredies as a flavouring, souring agent. By itself it is rarely used, for its taste is far too sharp and acid, even when braised or stewed, to make a good puree. The old-fashioned sailors' *moes*, or pottage, was made by stewing wild sorrel with whatever garden herbs were available and a little salt and fat into a thick, pasty brew, to which a little rice flour was usually added. It was eaten with a spoon. It tastes very much like hotel spinach, but is decidedly more aromatic and much more acid.

A somewhat similar concoction of indigenous spinach-like plants is made by the Africans and eaten as a relish with their mieliemeal porridge. It is reputed to be exceedingly vitamin-ish, but that consolation will certainly not debar the good cook from damning it.

Jakalskos is really the seed capsule of a parasitic plant, with curious, foul-smelling flowers, that grows on the roots of certain indigenous shrubs. In appearance it looks like a small, elongated coconut, with a rough dark-brown rind. Inside are found many tiny seeds embedded in a sweetish, aromatic, yellow pulp. It is usually partly covered with sand, and must be carefully looked for. Animals are fond of it and root up all they can find. It is therefore a rare thing at the best, and also exceedingly local. The pulp is scooped out, beaten up with a glass of sherry and some grated nutmeg and a little honey, and is served as a cold custard.

Baroe and kameroe are underground tubers that sometimes attain the size of a football. They are baked under the ashes or in the oven, like sweet potatoes, and eaten with salt and pepper. Boiled, they are starchy, insipid and need a great deal of spicing and flavouring; even then the result is not worth the trouble. They are best made into a preserve, by boiling them in a thin syrup with peach ker-

nels, ginger and a few featherings of cinnamon, when **veldkos**
their crispness and faintly-bitter taste can be duly appreciated.

The turgid underground rootstocks of *wild fennel* and
wild anise can be eaten raw for they are fairly sweet, with
a pungent, aromatic flavour. By themselves they make an
indifferent dish when boiled or stewed, for their flavour
is far too intense and does not seem to be influenced by
spicing. They make an excellent preserve which, like that
made from *baroe*, is characterised by a delicious crispness, a tinge of acidity, and an agreeable aromatic flavour.

Ghoo is the fruit of the wild almond tree, and in appearance and size resembles a large almond. The husk, and
to some extent the kernel also, contains a water-soluble
cyanide salt that is decomposed by heat. The fresh *ghoo*
"bean" is therefore very poisonous; a couple of the raw
kernels when eaten have been known to cause death. In
practice the husks are removed and the kernels are placed
in a sack which is put in running water for a week or more;
at the end of the time they are fit for use.

They are roasted like coffee beans, in a pot with a little
fat, and are then pounded into a powder, from which a
drink like cocoa is made. This is known as *ghoo coffee*,
and is an agreeable, refreshing and stimulating drink,
especially when prepared with milk. Boiled in water,
without previous roasting, the ghoo beans are reputed to
be extraordinarily nourishing; it is alleged that when the
Grey's Pass was under construction, the road gangs lived
mostly on ghoo beans and a wine ration and did better
work than anywhere else. Such boiled ghoo beans are
practically tasteless; to make them palatable, they are
mixed with spices and salt, pounded and made into a
puree, when their flavour is not unlike that of boiled pea-
nuts.

Little need be said of the indigenous fruits and berries,
some of which we will meet again when we deal with
sweet dishes. The veld around Cape Town used to provide several species of edible berries that were in demand
for sauces and garnishings, but today one must go much
farther afield to get them. *Kei-apple jelly*, made from the
fruit of a plant that is used for hedges, is one of the most
attractive-coloured jellies, with a bitter sour taste not
unlike a Seville marmalade. *Kaffir plum jam* and *stamvrug
jelly* are much more rarely met with, but are both excellent,
each with its strong individual taste.

117

Chapter XI

EGG DISHES

IN Cape cookery egg dishes are prepared from the eggs of domestic fowls, ducks, peahens, turkeys, geese, ostriches and guinea fowl, and from those of the wild duck, bustard, plover, mollymawk and penguin. While in general the egg recipes are imitations and variants of older European ones, there are some that show interesting modifications.

Early visitors to the Cape — like De la Caille (who had the entree to fashionable houses and could esteem the refinements of Cape cookery), Kolben (whose taste was of the pothouse variety), and Mentzel (who was much milder in his judgements about food, and who extolled the cleanliness and art of the Chinese eating houses that in his day were to be found in the neighbourhood of the docks) — wrote in praise of the egg cooking that they sampled. One of the earliest, a surgeon returning from India, tells us how in a "free burgher's" cottage he was treated to "a shapeless omelet, exquisitely made with crab". We may take it that what the gentleman so much enjoyed was a "fish with eggs", of which a recipe has already been given, made with pounded crayfish instead of fish.

I have been unable to trace, in print, the earliest mention of penguin eggs, but there is no doubt that they were used in Van Riebeeck's time. In my youth they were quite common and cheap on the Cape Town market; since they came under bureaucratic control they have become scarce, almost unobtainable, and very expensive.

As a delicacy "Malagas eggs" were regarded as superior; plovers eggs, that could sometimes be bought, were not reckoned anything to be proud of; their flavour was said to be inferior to that of a Malagas egg. Wild duck eggs, bustard eggs (*korhaan eiers*) and, very rarely, crane's or heron's eggs, could on occasion also be bought

118

at the market. One of my earliest recollections is that of **eggs** being treated to half a pelican's egg, hard boiled, by the late Mr Saul Solomon, the locally-renowned liberal orator, at his house at Sea Point. As I remember, its flavour was harsher than that of a penguin's egg and its delicacy was not to be compared with that of a Malagas egg.

Turtle and tortoises eggs were also sometimes to be had; the former were always snapped up by the Government House steward, who was said to have a private method of preserving them, probably by packing them in coarse salt in an earthenware jar. Ostrich eggs — at first always from wild birds, but in the middle of the past century almost exclusively from the domesticated ostriches — were sold for a few pence each, but were regarded as coarse.

Fowls eggs, always easily obtainable, were sometimes as cheap as four pennies a dozen, and their cheapness no doubt encouraged the cooks to experiment in many ways to improve them for the table. There were already hundreds of recipes; no one has attempted to count how many different ways there are of dealing with eggs, but at a guess there must be more than half a thousand; and among so many directives it is inevitable that there should be a certain amount of overlapping.

Boiled eggs: My old preceptress, who emphasised her injunctions with good-natured taps of her wooden spoon on my head, insisted that penguin eggs should be boiled in sea water, steadily for 15 minutes. That produced a clear, transparent jelly surrounding an opalescent green yolk that crumbled readily to fine primrose-yellow flaky fragments, for nobody ever ate them soft-boiled.

Fowls eggs, for soft boiling, were put into cold water which was brought to the boil, when the eggs were taken out; if they were wanted hard-boiled, the ebullition was allowed to proceed for three or more minutes. If you wanted a crumbly yolk, that could be made almost into a powder, you boiled th egg for half an hour; then, according to the Ayah, you could preserve the eggs for several weeks by merely storing them in a jar of slightly salted water.

Among her favourite breakfast dishes were the following:

Orange eggs. Select a large, not too ripe, seedling orange (she invariably chose the Clanwilliam variety, which has a very thin skin and is grandly juicy), cut it in half, remove the pips, and scoop out a little of the pulp; sprinkle with salt, break into each half a newly-laid egg, dust with salt and pepper, and bake in the oven till the egg is nicely set.

She varied this by using avocado pears, large tomatoes, small squashes, baked potatoes, even small melons first sprinkled with grated nutmeg, salt and a few drops of rum.

More elaborately, she made:

119

eggs   *Eggs on bacon.* Chop up fat bacon; braise it with some chillies, a teaspoonful of chutney, minced onion and powdered ginger. Put it in a buttered shell (she used a small pearl mussel shell, which makes a good ramekin mould) break an egg on it, dust with salt and pepper and bake till set.

Crayfish egg. Pound some of the soft, greenish-white flesh found adhering to the inner part of the carapace of a boiled crayfish with some salt, ginger powder, boiled egg yolk and some of the coral. Put in a small buttered pan; break an egg on it, and stand it in a vessel of boiling water till the egg is lightly set; dust with nutmeg and serve.

For a foundation she sometimes used finely-shredded fried snoek, pounded *bokkom* braised in a little butter with a few shreds of onion and a suspicion of garlic, or simply breadcrumbs soaked in a rich gravy and, to add piquancy, she sometimes mixed these combinations with a little curry sauce. Her generic name for these various very tasty dishes was *eiers met iets onder* (eggs with something underneath).

Similarly, she was fertile in her expedients to sophisticate her plain hard-boiled eggs. She halved and curried them, allowing them to simmer gently for a few minutes in a rich curry sauce, and serving them up with plain boiled dry rice. She took out the yolks, pounded them with spices, bits of fried fish, crayfish coral, or minced herbs, onion and lemon juice, replacing them neatly within the severed white and serving them with a sour sauce.

With ostrich eggs, an expert cook can have a positive holiday. The first thing to be done is to get at the contents of the shell. One makes a hole at the top end, and by gently shaking the shell the fluid white and yolk may be persuaded to run into a basin; it is almost impossible, by ordinary methods, to separate the white from the yellow. For that reason the most popular way of serving an ostrich egg – which by itself is the equal of more than a dozen hens eggs – is to whip what comes down into the basin, and to cook it as:

Volstruiseierstruif (scrambled ostrich egg). Mix the whipped egg with a little minced onion, salt and pepper; melt a large lump of butter or fat in a pan; when it begins to brown, stir in the eggs; continue stirring till it is set; serve piled on a dish well dusted with salt and pepper.

This gives a rather watery, almost pasty result which it seems impossible to correct except by allowing the egg, before it is whipped, to stand in a cool place overnight, and before using it, to separate the top portion and scramble what remains. Even then, and even by using plenty of butter, it is not easy to get the rich flakiness of buttered eggs. The scrambled egg may be much improved by the addition of grated cheese. At a pinch one can make a heavy omelet with ostrich egg, but its taste and flavour

120

are inferior to anything made from hens eggs.

The best use for ostrich egg is as an egg substitute in baked cakes and puddings, where its coarse flavour is moderately well disguised. Old cooks used to boil the whole egg, for half an hour or more, till it was well set. It was then shelled, cut into slices and used to decorate vegetable salads. In the early printed cookery books (not in any of my manuscripts) may be found a curious recipe for preparing an *imitation ostrich egg*, by covering an orange-sized ball of pounded and cooked chicken meat, boiled egg yolk, spices and saffron, with a thick layer of a paste made with a white sauce and rice powder and steaming it in a round mould.

Penguin eggs are best served plainly hard-boiled in their shells. At table they are shelled, mashed up with a fork (that nearly always gets discoloured in the process) mixed with salt and pepper and a few drops of vinegar or lemon juice, and eaten with bread and butter. They may be made into scrambled or buttered eggs, served with a curry sauce, creamed, combined with anchovies or flaked fried fish, or covered with a cheese sauce. None of these can compare with the simple hard-boiled egg, which has always been considered a delicacy, although some people consider it overrated.

Gulls and mollymawks eggs are by some connoisseurs more highly-prized than penguin eggs. They should be simply boiled and eaten with a little salt, pepper and vinegar.

Chapter XII

GAME AND
CAMP COOKERY

WHEN one considers the fact that the first settlers found South Africa teeming with game, it is surprising that the development of game cookery proceeded comparatively slowly. The manuscript recipes show no important modifications from the already known directives for the preparation of the flesh of wild animals that appeared in the printed cook books of the seventeenth century. The reason for this is probably the scarcity of game in the East with, as a consequence, the neglect of Malay cooks to deal with foodstuffs that were new to them. It may also be on account of the relative scarcity of game at the settlement itself.

During the first 50 years game was undoubtedly plentiful in the environs of Cape Town, but it soon became so scarce that the prices in the open market were increased beyond the capacity of the pockets of most of the burghers. Mentzel, much later, records that the four huntsmen, who were the only people allowed to shoot game, could hardly get enough to satisfy the requirements of the Governor's household. While this is undoubtedly an exaggeration, and while a great deal of poaching must have occurred, it is clear that game was not a common foodstuff in poor or middle-class homes. It was prepared for the table in accordance with the recipes derived from Europe, and there are very few modifications of these that show a decided Oriental or local influence.

There has existed, however, from very early times what **game** may be called an oral traditional repository of directions for cooking game that was preserved, augmented and improved by all those who were in a position where such game supplied their daily needs. These guardians were the hunters. First those who went out in small parties, camped on the veld for a few nights, and returned to the settlement and, later on, those who adventured, with or without their families, far beyond the limits of civilisation. The methods that they used were rough and ready, but were influenced by age old principles of gipsy cookery, probably imported by servants of the Company who had experience of improvised camp cooking in the south of Europe where the Romany way of broiling under ashes and cooking in a covering of clay was still adhered to.

Much of it was forgotten in the Cape Colony, but it was remembered by those who went beyond the Vaal river and today it exists, in a modified form, in the Transvaal, where it is actively honoured by all those who have the leisure and inclination to indulge in that delightful avocation, camping in the Bushveld.

A glance through the old European cookery books shows at once that many of their recipes for game dishes are useless in South Africa simply because we have not got the necessary ingredients. We have no pheasants (ours are all partridges) no ortolans, ptarmigans, rabbits (except at Robben Island, whence one seldom gets an eatable one) ; and we disdain to use, except in our early, nursery years, sparrows and suchlike small fry. On the other hand, we have a number of excellent game animals and of others that, although they are not classed as game, are not only eatable but very good eating indeed, of whose existence the old Italian cooks had no knowledge. We have no chance of eating swans, but we have the flamingo, whose flesh is incomparably superior ; our quails are in season extraordinarily fat and succulent ; our snipe, ground partridges, and go-away birds vie with any ortolan or golden plover in Europe. We have a variety of wild buck, among which the eland, springbok, duiker and steenbok give us venison that is superior in quality to anything that Europe can produce.

So great is the variety of our wild animals that the cook in dealing with their flesh will find ample opportunity to exercise his ingenuity, to improvise where necessary, and to modify the old recipes in conformity to modern taste.

It is perhaps better to deal with each variety separately, but before doing so it is desirable to say a few words about the general methods used in South African camp cookery.

No camping outfit is considered complete without the stewpot, which is a round iron receptacle, with a well fitting lid, standing on three spiked feet, which is known as the *drievoetpot* or tripod pot. Its capacity varies from a gallon to three or more, and it is usually swung, with the iron kettle, under the ox-wagon, though today it goes into the baggage compartment of the car. A frying pan and a gridiron are also required. The range and variety of

game equipment will, of course, depend on the size of the camping party and the particular whimsies of individual shots or cooks, but the four utensils mentioned are essential.

The iron pot is used for stewing, boiling, and simmering; the pan for shallow frying, for pancakes, and for making special sauces; the gridiron for grilling; the kettle is solely for boiling water for coffee or tea.

Milk is almost never boiled in camp; indeed it is rarely used, except when it can be obtained locally, for condensed or dried milk serves equally well. Water sometimes has to be filtered before it can be used; green vegetables are scarce, but spices and dried herbs are brought with the groceries and the camp cook generally has no need to stint himself; he can even get excellent flavourings by walking a few yards out of camp and picking the leaves of wild plants. Usually an oven is made by scooping a hole in an ant hill, which is heated by burning wood inside; the loaves are placed in it as in an ordinary oven and the entrance is closed. Damper is made in the usual way and either grilled on the gridiron or baked under the ashes.

We may now proceed to consider the several varieties of wild animals that may require the cook's attention.

Pigeons: The large rock pigeon and the two kinds of green pigeon are the only ones generally used, though the ordinary turtle dove, the rameron and the speckled dove are also good eating. The green pigeon, especially in the summer when it has fed on wild figs, is tender, aromatic, and fat; it needs no larding. In camp it is stewed, cooked with other game as a ragout, or grilled. The old recipes for pigeons include the following:

Pigeons with crayfish. Salt and pepper the carcase inside and out and stuff with pounded crayfish mixed with ginger, mace, marjoram, pepper and salt; if you like, you may add a little pounded chilli; stew gently in white wine, keeping the pot closely covered. Serve with wet rice.

Stuffed pigeons. Remove the backbone and breastbone; carefully remove as much meat from the bird as you can get out without breaking the skin; pound this in a mortar with a little marrow or suet, lemon peel, parsley, bread crumbs and a little cream; add the yolk of an egg and a few shreds of anchovy. Fill the skin of the pigeon with this, and sew it up; place in a pot with some sliced onion, a little fat pork and a cupful of wine, and simmer gently, without allowing it to brown. Place on a dish, thicken the sauce with a glass of sherry and some arrowroot, pour over and serve with wet rice.

Pigeon stew (camp style). Cut the pigeons into quarters and put in the pot with any herbs or spices you may have, adding fat and chopped pork or game fat. Let it slowly simmer with the lid on, till tender; then add salt and pepper, a cupful of wine, or water if you have no wine, and let it simmer gently for several hours.

It is better when the pigeons are married, in the pot, to

124

some other game, bird or mammal. At home the dish is game finished by adding boiling cream, thickening the sauce, and stirring in breadcrumbs.

Quails: Deal with them as you would with pigeons. Or stuff them with any of the fillings mentioned in the chapter on meat; wrap them in fig or vine leaves, and stew them slowly in white wine. They are usually fat enough when in season to be cooked without larding or a wrapper of bacon.

Snipe and small game birds are treated in the same way, but the old Malay cooks eviscerated them only when they wished to stuff them; ordinarily they were not drawn, but enclosed in a mantle of fat pork and gently simmered with spices and herbs, and finished off with a dash of sherry. The small plovers are excellent when done in this manner.

Bustards: These range from the royal *gom pou* (otis kori) that weighs as much as 60 lb., to the various species of *korhaans* and *dikkops* averaging a few pounds in weight when drawn and cleaned. They are cooked exactly like a muscovy duck – that is, stuffed with some kind of filling, covered with fat pork and pot-roasted or stewed. In camp they are camp-stewed by themselves or with other birds or game. They are excellent eating, and usually require no larding, but as they are protected game, one rarely has a chance to taste them.

Flamingo, too, is "royal game", and cannot be shot. Formerly it was obtainable, though not easily, and I have eaten it on several occasions, and personally approved the two following recipes:

Flamingo supreme (flaminkbors). Remove the breast meat; cut it into neat strips; beat each with a wooden mallet; roll in pepper and salt; place in red wine and let them lie for a couple of hours. Take out, wipe dry and place in a pot with diced pork fat, a blade of mace, a lemon leaf, a sprig of thyme, and a few peppercorns and cardamons; add a few spoonfuls of wine, and let it stew gently with the lid on. Take out and place on your serving dish; thicken the gravy with flour, stir in a glass of brandy or sweet wine and a tablespoonful of lemon juice; pour over and serve.

Stuffed breast of flamingo. Carefully remove the flesh from both sides of the breastbone, and place it in red wine for a couple of hours; wipe dry and rub in pepper and salt and a little pounded chilli. Take a fairly coherent farce; mould it to fit the inside of the two breast pieces; wrap them round the farce and skewer with wooden pegs or bind with string. Put in a saucepan with a few cups of red wine, a bit of lemon peel or scented verbena, a few cloves and a handful of small onions. Let it simmer gently till tender; thicken the gravy with a white sauce and serve.

Flamingo flesh is equally good when simply shallow-fried in a little fat with pepper and salt. It is, of all bird

125

game flesh, perhaps the most tender, tasty and delicately flavoured, possibly because the bird feeds on an aquatic,
plankton diet that imparts to its meat an extraordinarily
savoury quality. An early Cape traveller maintained that
soup made from it was claret coloured, but this is a mistake; the flesh is dark, like that of a duck, but contains no
pigment of any kind; when grilled, it is practically
indistinguishable from beef as far as colour is concerned,
but its tenderness is far superior and it seldom needs
larding.

Herons and *cranes* are still sometimes sold by the
butchers. They are prepared for the table like ducks, and
are good eating, although they need larding and prolonged
stewing, in bouillon or wine. The blue crane is considered
the best; its flesh is dark, aromatic and delicate; its liver,
broiled, is a delicious titbit, comparable to that of the
muscovy duck.

Wild duck, waterfowl: Of these there are several
varieties, none of which is equal to the domestic species,
and some of which have a pronounced oily, almost rank
taste. Recipes for their preparation follow the oldest one
in the cookery books, and no modification that is known
to me is of practical importance.

Partridges. There are several kinds, ranging from the
larger ones, equal in size to a domestic fowl, to the small
swempie that weighs a few ounces, but is perhaps the
best eating of all. From a gastronomic point of view their
excellence varies considerably; sometimes one gets a
partridge that is everything one can wish it to be; the
next day one may have another of the same kind, prepared
in exactly the same way, that is tasteless and insipid.
The difference probably depends on the diet of the bird.
One gets partridges that have a distinct aromatic flavour,
sometimes very strong, reminiscent of mint or sage, and
it is likely that these birds have fed on wild plants. At home
all partridges need larding or at least swathing in bacon
or fat pork, and can be prepared in accordance with the
many recipes in the books.

The old manuscripts give the following directions for
making:

Hunters bredie. Take cleaned and drawn partridge, and a
couple or more cleaned pigeons or any other wild fowl.
Wipe them well, and rub inside and outside with pepper
and salt. Put them in an iron pot, and lay on them strips of
fat pork; add a few spoonfuls of fat, put the lid on, and let
it stew slowly and gently; you may put some hot coals on
the lid, and from time to time you must stir the contents,
but you must not add water. Take care that it does not
burn. Simmer it till the flesh falls off the bones, and serve
in the pot.

That is the camp way. At home, one would add mace,
coriander seeds, a shred of chilli and perhaps a few herb
leaves. The result in both cases should be a whitish-grey,
slightly pasty but exceedingly succulent stew. The
method of making it is known as *rafeltjieskook* or

"stewing to shreds", and is excellent for partridges, hares **game** and smaller buck.

Kwe-bird or *go-away-bird* is a sub-tropical loerie of an ash-grey colour with a crest that it can raise or depress at will. In summer when it feeds on the highly-aromatic Bushveld berries its flesh, which when stewed is as tender as marrow, is beautifully aromatic. As it is a comparatively small bird, half a dozen of its supremes or breast fillets are required to make a satisfactory dish. They are best simply stewed in fat, need neither larding nor spicing, and are just as good when they are grilled. Only private enterprise will obtain them.

Hare. The recipes for this animal's appearance on the dinner table are obviously cribbed from European textbooks; the main modification when stewing it is to do so without adding a drop of water as in the hunter's stew. This yields a fragrant, succulent and tasty dish, which is always served with wet rice and something sweet to accompany it. Another modification is that of the old fashioned Dutch ragout known as *hasepeper*, in which the animal is cut up, stewed in wine, with herbs and spices, to which, when the stewing is nearly done, a cupful of its blood is added, beaten up with some vinegar or tamarind juice. The gravy is allowed to simmer for a little while longer, and small dumplings of forcemeat or of the hare's liver are added; finally a little arrowroot is stirred in, and the ragout is served with wet rice.

In passing it may be mentioned that game was considered unfit for cooking if it was "high"; it was allowed to hang for a few days, but in general cooks preferred to deal with it when it was moderately-fresh, and some used it as soon as it was killed. To prevent tainting, it was salted and wind-dried. The old recipes give directions for "removing any smell from game bought at the market". This was not always successful, for Mentzel complains that some of the venison he tasted was not as fresh as it might have been. Nowadays moderately-high game is not objected to, although something less odoriferous is usually preferred.

Wild buck: There are so many varieties that one can merely give a paragraph to some of the more easily obtainable ones. The manner of serving them is practically the same in all cases. In camp the meat, by itself or with the addition of wild birds or other meat, is put in the stewpot, with pepper, salt and plenty of fat, and allowed to simmer for many hours, practically for the whole day. The result is a perfect pot-roast, if the meat has been allowed to cook by itself, or a fragrant stew if it is a mixture. Sometimes potatoes or other vegetables are added a couple of hours before the meat is served. At home a grander ritual is followed.

Leg of game. Wash and dry it; lard it well with pork fat cut into narrow strips; rub in with salt, pepper, crushed coriander seed, brown sugar and a little chilli. Put the meat in vinegar to which you have added a cup of red wine; let it lie there for three days, turning it each day; if

127

game you like you may add to the marinade a couple of crushed
bay or lemon leaves. On the fourth day take out, wipe and
dry; dust with fine flour; put in a pan with plenty of fat,
and let it roast; baste frequently with the butter and, when
it begins to brown, baste with the marinade. When tender,
take out, brush egg white over and place in the oven; boil
the gravy and add to it a glass of sweet wine, pepper, salt
and grated nutmeg, boil up, thicken with roux and serve
with the roast.

With this one served wet rice, sweet potatoes and usually
a salad. Some, however, served stewed fruit with it.

Fillets of game. Cut neat, regularly-shaped fillets from
the neck or back portion of the buck (the best is from the
muscles that lie along the spinal column), rub in salt,
pepper and a little sifted flour; simmer in fat with a pinch
of powdered ginger; make a good gravy sauce, and add to
it lemon juice, chilli, a little sweet red wine and enough
rice flour to thicken it. Dip the stewed fillets in lemon juice
and powder them with pepper and salt; put them in a
shallow dish; pour over the boiling gravy sauce and serve.

The largest of the antelopes in South Africa is the *eland*.
Its flesh, especially the hump, is savoury and tender, and
needs no larding. It is usually pot-roasted, but can be
prepared in all the various ways that are used for beef.

The next largest antelopes are the *kudu* and the
hartebeest whose flesh is far inferior to that of the
eland although, when properly prepared, kudu steak and
fillet, well larded, are tasty enough. Of the other antelopes,
the larger *wildebeest* or *gnu* is the most common; its
meat is tasteless and stringy, but its tongue, liver, brains,
and kidneys are considered delicacies. *Reedbuck* or
impala, *springbok*, *blesbuck* and the smaller *steen*, *grys*
and *ribbok* are much better; their meat is generally tender, faintly aromatic and, although they all need larding,
their venison is excellent. It is largely used to make biltong,
being slightly salted, cut into narrow strips and dried in the
open air. The legs and shoulders of the smaller kinds are immersed in salt-salpetre-spice marinade, and are then
sundried as *wildsboutjies*, the meat becoming less dry
than true game biltong, so that it can be cut into thin
slices which are eaten like beef biltong. Today venison,
usually springbok or blesbuck, can be obtained out of
season from cold storage depots, but is never so good as
when obtained in camp.

Hippopotamus meat was formerly obtainable at the
Cape Town market. At the earliest public market it was
sold at two pence a pound. Today it is to be obtained
only beyond the borders of our country, and there are few
people who have tasted it. It has a peculiar flavour, inter-
mediate between that of pork and beef, a slightly pasty
consistency from its superfluity of fat between the muscle
fibres, and a tough fascial layer over the soft parts that
must be removed before it can be cooked. The breast and
back muscles are reputed to be the best and choicest
bits; they are pot-roasted with spices and herbs and are

128

regarded as the greatest delicacies that the hunter can **game** provide. Even when cooked in this way, the meat is apt to be greasy; it certainly needs the addition of wine or vinegar to improve it.

Giraffe meat is coarse and stringy, but parts of it are excellent, and the long, succulent tongue, properly cooked is not only eatable but delectable. The expectant cook will be much disappointed to learn that the animal's well-developed bones are quite useless for marrow bones; with every care, all that results when such a bone is boiled or baked, is a mess of yellow, unappetising oil that cannot be coaxed to a consistency that will enable it to adjust itself to a piece of toast.

Zebra flesh, on the other hand, I should without hesitation deem the tenderest, most savoury, and best flavoured of all game meat, especially when the animal is young. A zebra fillet, portioned into tournedos, is incomparably the finest meat that is obtainable in a Bushveld camp. It needs no preliminary marinading and is perhaps better without any sophistication. All that is necessary is to cut it into suitable pieces, pepper and salt it, after, perhaps, rubbing it all over with the aromatic leaves of some veld shrub like *blinkblaar*, and frying it in its own fat (which is of a deep chrome yellow colour) and serving it with its gravy thickened with a little flour and sherry.

Its succulent tenderness and its delicious flavour are a revelation to those who have never tried it, and it is astonishing that there still remains a prejudice against eating it. There is no reason whatever for this absurd distaste, for the animal is a clean grass feeder, is generally when shot in prime condition, and has no smell of any kind.

Among the earliest manuscript recipes for preparing wild animals for the table is one that gives directions for cooking:

Porcupine crackling. Plunge the animal, as you would a sucking pig, into boiling water; scrape off the pens and the hairs; scrub the skin till it is perfectly smooth and white. Now skin the animal and discard the meat, which is not very nice to eat. Put the skin in a jar in salt water to which you have added a little vinegar, and let it lie in it overnight. Take it out the next day, dry it, rub it with a clove of garlic and put it in a saucepan with a little boiling water. Boil till it is tender enough to allow a fork to pierce it easily. Take it out and cut it up into pieces about the size of flattened apricots (about two inches square) which you may either grill or fry in a pan with a little fat. Put on the pieces some pepper and salt and send to table with plenty of rice, and lemons cut in halves.

This out-of-the-way dish would have delighted Elia, for its sapid crispness far exceeds that of ordinary pork crackling.

Roast leguan. Take only the white flesh; cut it into thick strips, which you must powder with salt and chillies, and

game then put into a pan with some fat, a few coriander seeds, parsley leaves and a teaspoonful of chutney sauce. Put the lid on and simmer slowly till the meat is tender. Add a teaspoonful of China (soya) sauce and let it simmer for a few minutes more. Arrange the meat on a dish; thicken the sauce with a little roux, pour over and serve.

Leguans used to be obtainable on the Pretoria market, where there was a good demand for them from Chinese customers. Their meat is excellent when done in this way, without the slightest trace of any rankness or objectionable flavour, rather like chicken meat though of a more robust quality.

Elephant meat: This, too, the ordinary diner will not get a chance of sampling. On safari most of it is given to the camp followers. The foot, baked in an improvised oven or under the ashes, is regarded by many as a delicacy, but actually it has little to commend it, though a competent cook could no doubt make it into a palatable dish. The average man will probably much prefer sheep's trotters prepared in one of the conventional ways.

Python: Several kinds of snakes are eaten, not usually, however, by Europeans. The flesh of the python is tender, savoury and like that of a well-fed pig, but is generally so fat that it needs preliminary broiling, to separate from it some of its oily extravagance. It can then be roasted in a pot in the ordinary manner.

Selous, and other hunters, state that *lion* meat is as palatable as that of buck, and on several occasions, in Bushveld camps, I have confirmed this opinion by preparing the meat in various ways. It is best fried as steaks, after marinading in wine and vinegar. When stewed it is apt to be insipid, though it is rarely stringy or tough. It makes excellent biltong of a delicate pinkish colour which, when grated, is hardly to be distinguished from buck biltong. The prejudice against using it is, however, so inveterate that the carcase of a lion or lioness, when the skin has been taken off, is either handed to the natives, who regard particular parts of it as tit-bits, or boiled to extract the fat for soap making.

There are several recipes for dealing with *tortoises*. These animals are still common in Bushmanland and the Bushveld, and some species yield several pounds of good meat, which must be extracted by chopping open the shell or, preferably, after boiling the animal rapidly until the shell falls to pieces.

Stewed tortoise. Take out the flesh carefully, taking care not to break the gall bladder. Separate it from the bones and gristly parts, and cut it up into neat pieces. Place them in the pot, with a little fat, a tablespoonful of sifted flour, salt, pepper and such herbs as are available, and allow to simmer gently, till tender. Thicken the gravy with breadcrumbs; add a wineglass of wine and serve.

At home, powdered ginger, a pinch of chilli, and a few tablespoonfuls of a good stock are added, and the meat allowed to stew. Then a large tablespoonful of lemon

juice is stirred in, and the stewing is continued for another
15 minutes. The meat is taken out, arranged on a dish, and
the gravy to which a cup of boiling cream has been added,
is poured over it. It is generally eaten with wet rice and
some sweet dish, either stewed fruit or sweet potatoes.

Tortoise in jelly. A rich jelly is made with seaweed
boiled in a strong bouillon; a greased mould is coated
with this, and sliced hard boiled eggs are set in the
coating when it is nearly stiff. Then follows a layer of
braised tortoise meat, with pepper and salt, and preserved,
pickled gherkins, sliced length-wise. The remainder of the
jelly is poured over and the mould is put in a cool place till
the contents are firm. It is then turned out on a layer of
lettuce leaves, garnished with young radishes and carrots
and served with a sour sauce.

Tortoise in its shell. The meat is taken out carefully and
cut into small pieces, which are braised in fat with a little
onion, a clove of garlic, a crushed chilli and some salt.
The shell is carefully cleaned, its inside rubbed with fat and
it is filled with the braised meat, mixed with bread crumbs
steeped in milk, and a cup of orange juice. It is put in the
oven and baked and served with rice and chutney.

Creamed tortoise. The meat is carefully cut up into
comparatively small pieces, all the gristle being rejected. It
is then simmered in white wine, with a little white pepper,
powdered ginger and a blade of mace. When tender, salt is
added, and a cup of boiling cream, which is allowed to
thicken before the dish is served. Some cooks add a handful of white crumbs pressed out in milk.

Wild pig: The warthog and the bushpig are plentiful
in certain parts of the Bushveld, and their meat is appre-

game ciated by both Europeans and Africans. It differs so much from pork in its flavour and texture that those who taste it for the first time will probably be unaware that they are eating pig's meat. All the recipes that apply to pork can be used for warthog and bushpig meat.

There remain some odd dishes, whose recipes cannot be found in old manuscripts but are enshrined in oral tradition. Every good cook knows about them for, as a master of the craft has expressed it, "some of the tastiest concoctions cannot be served at an ordinary dinner, just as some of a juggler's best tricks cannot be shown before a large audience." Here are a few for whose excellence I can vouch:

Baked ox head. An ox head, neatly trimmed so that it can stand upright on the neck part, is washed and scrubbed without removing any hair. Particular attention should be given, in this cleansing process, to the nostrils, ears and eyelids. The horns should not be removed. The whole head is placed in a large bread oven, and left there to bake for a day and a night. It is then allowed to get cold and replaced in the oven where it undergoes a further prolonged baking. When it is tender, it is taken out, put upright on a large salver and served just as it comes from the oven. The carver cuts through and reflects the skin from the forehead and cheeks, and serves to each guest some part of the underlying fat, a bit of the tongue, palate, or whatever is fancied.

One's first emotion, on seeing this immense and horrific roast – in which, if the head happens to be that of an Afrikaner ox, the horns appear to stretch the whole length of the dining table, while the baked eyes stare with an expression that is ludicrous as well as baleful, and the lips are drawn back to show the teeth in a sort of snarl that no living ox ever shows – is one of profound shock. Indeed, on the first occasion when I assisted, as General Botha's guest, at a party where this gruesome dish was the main and only item on the bill of fare, two of my fellow gourmets were so overcome that they had to leave the table.

Yet barbecued in this fashion, the fleshy parts of the head are exquisitely tender, as sapid as the meat of a young partridge, with a flavour that no beef can excel. As absolutely no condiments have been used in preparing the meat, each guest salts and peppers his portion at table according to his own taste. One is supposed to eat it with "wet" rice, but any vegetable goes well with it and personally, I have found it delicious when eaten with a plain salad.

It is, of course, a dish that cannot be ordinarily presented and there is no reason why it should not be made more attractive, if less imposing, by cutting off the horns, sewing up the eyelids and lips, and removing the hair before it is baked, but tradition insists that the way described is the only right way in which it should be cooked, served and eaten. And once one has tasted it,

132

the memory of its surpassing succulence remains with **game** one, just as the recollection of the bouquet, aroma and savour of an exquisite wine lingers through the years, stimulating the longing for a repetition of so perfect an experience in degustation.

From the sublime to the ridiculous one steps when, after tasting this delicious monstrosity, one is invited to eat:

Fried locusts. Nip off their wings, heads and legs, after you have plunged them into boiling water mercifully to kill them. What remains are the thorax and abdomen, which are the only parts that interest the epicure. You dust them with a mixture of pepper and salt (to which for some absurd reason that I have never been able to understand, some people add a little powdered cinnamon) and shallow-fry them in fat till they are crisp and brown. They taste not unlike whitebait that, somehow, have been stuffed with buttered toast.

Less unconformable are some of the more common dishes that one tastes in camp. Made at home they would be finished off in the usual way in which skilled cooks give to their concoctions — just that inimitable turn that converts the ordinary into the best — but made in the traditional fashion, with the means that are available, and cooked by the slow, prolonged, cumulative application of heat, and eaten when one's appetite has been sharpened by a day's exercise in the open air, they are hard to surpass. The essence of their goodness lies in the slowness with which they have been cooked; any hurry in their preparation ends in something which it is hardly worthwhile to eat, except for the sordid purpose of satisfying hunger.

Camp soup. The large thigh bones of some of the bigger buck, containing marrow and having still on them some scraps of meat, are cut in half and placed in a large pot, which is filled with cold water. To them are added pieces of game, a generous portion of salt fat pork, a few handfuls of dried beans, peas and any vegetables that are to be had, such as carrots, potatoes, and onions, and finally a handful of coarse salt. The lid is placed on the pot, which is then stood over the fire, where it is allowed to boil gently the whole day long. It is frequently stirred, some pepper and whatever condiments — sometimes a few tablespoonfuls of some bottled sauce — are available are added. In the evening the pot is placed where it can be heated by the camp fire. Its contents now are of the consistency of a wellmade Italian *minestra*, but as a soup it is infinitely superior, though perhaps too rich, in a proud, even aggressive way, for in it float large lumps of marrow and over it half an inch of oil. Part of the supernatant oil is skimmed off; the rest is stirred into the potage when each member of the party dips into it with the ladle to fill his soup plate or pannikin and to select scraps of meat for individual consumption.

133

game This soup, which is something more than a soup and not quite a stew, is so luscious and filling that when eaten with a piece of bread or damper, one needs little after it. Its ingredients have been so well blended that the liquid portion (sometimes so strong that if strained and set aside it jellies into a delicious bouillon) is a fragrant, well-flavoured, rich thick soup, while the solid constituents are thoroughly impregnated with its savouriness. There is usually enough boiled marrow floating in the soup for each guest to get a fair share of it, and generally so much meat that the greater part of it returns to the camp kitchen to be consumed by the native cook and his retinue.

Camp sausage: Meat left over from the biltong making is passed through the mincing machine (in the old days it was pounded in a wooden mortar). Several varieties of game meat mixed make the best sausage meat, to which must be added pork or game fat cut into dice, salt, plenty of pepper and such spices as can be obtained or have been brought for the purpose. The sausage meat is kneaded with some vinegar and stuffed into the cleaned skins (entrails) which are then hung up for a few days. It may be dried again, to be eaten raw if desired, but more usually it is fried when still wet. The dried sausage will keep for months and, if soaked in a little salt water, can be used for frying or boiling.

Such game sausage is full-flavoured, and when it is to be fried it should be well pricked; the bits of diced fat within it give it enough lubricant for grilling on the gridiron. It is excellent when simply fried in the pan, but is not so good when boiled.

Some campers still make the old-fashioned *blood sausage* with game blood mixed with breadcrumbs, minced meat, diced pork, salt and pepper. This too, will keep, but is best used freshly made, when it is sliced and fried with fat in a pan.

Brain cakes. The brains of the buck are extracted, par-boiled, mixed with a little minced onion, salt and pepper, and baked in a pan with a little fat. Or they are shaped into thicker cakes and rolled in flour and then fried.

Another way to do them is to dip them in a fairly thick batter, and fry them in fat.

Partridge in clay. Let the partridge be freshly killed (game birds are never allowed to hang till they are high, although they are generally plucked and drawn immediately they are brought to camp — they are sometimes not cooked for a couple of days; if the weather is cool, that does not taint them) and do not draw or pluck it. Cut off its legs just below the feathered part, and its head at the top of the neck. Coat the bird with a thick layer of clay that you have made into a dough, so that it is wholly covered. Place it on hot coals and shovel coals and ashes over it, replenishing them when they are no longer hot. When the

134

clay has become hard and baked, rake out the bird and
let the clay get cold. Then crack it with a stone, take out
the partridge, and serve.

Most folk prefer to draw the bird before cooking it, but
the undrawn bird is certainly more savoury. If the clay
has been red hot, the feathers, and part of the skin of the
bird, will stick to the fragments ; the bird itself is cooked
to a turn, and magnificently tender and savoury ; all it
needs is a little salt and pepper.

Other wild animals can be cooked in the same way,
which is really an old Romany method of cooking. Apart
from this we have no proper barbecueing ways of preparing food, though the old fashion, followed by Apicius,
of baking foodstuffs under the hot ashes of a wood fire,
is conveniently honoured in camp. As has already been
mentioned, the ubiquitous ant-heap provides an admirable camp oven, in which practically anything can be
baked, either in a pan or wrapped in fig or paw-paw
leaves.

Whale flesh was, and still is, a common article of food
and is a most nourishing meat. So, too, is the flesh of the
walrus and the *seal*, both of which could be obtained
still at the end of the past century at the Cape Town fish
market. All these are coarse-grained, generally with much
fat between the muscle fibres, and with an oily taste
that is, however, effectually eliminated by proper preliminary marinading, and adequate spicing when pot-
roasted. A whale or walrus steak, grilled, is quite tender,
tasty and eatable, but it is coarse compared with a good
game or buck steak. Made into a stew, the way in which
the old fishermen preferred it, with potatoes and cabbage,
it is better. All three meats produce, when boiled, a very
savoury and exceedingly nourishing broth, but it must
be most carefully skimmed and flavoured, for its taste is
not to everyone's liking.

Chapter XIII

FRUITS AND SWEET DISHES

THE modern cook would find it difficult to make most of his sweet dishes if he were deprived of sugar and had to find an adequate substitute for it. Yet that was the difficulty that, 400 years ago, the old cooks successfully overcame. They had no sugar, but they used honey and the concentrated juice of sweet fruits, or the fruits themselves, to achieve results that we now would regard as unobtainable in the absence of sugar.

In our oldest recipes sugar is not mentioned; honey takes its place and is used in a manner that is no longer orthodox. For example, choice hams were preserved in honey; puddings and cakes, and even the first ices, were sweetened with it. The expressed sweet juice of the grape, the cherry and the plum was boiled, to make a concentrated syrup which was used when honey was not available.

The first colonists at the Cape had access to imported sugar, but it was an exceedingly scarce and expensive article, whose use became general only in the eighteenth century. It was imported in the form of a coarse, almost black, unrefined sugar from China; later on it came in as a partly-refined, but still very moist, yellow; and still later as a white sugar, or as candy sugar which was a mass of well defined crystals clustered round a bit of string. The early recipes give directions for powdering such candy sugar and also for "clearing" unrefined sugar, when **fruits** a transparent syrup was required for preserving fruit.

It is interesting to note that the quantities of sugar prescribed in those early days for the preparation of sweet dishes yield results that are much less sweet than what would be acceptable today, which may be either because the sugar then used, being unrefined, was more saccharine, or because (which is more probable) diners were content with a dish that was moderately sweet.

Another interesting point is that early Cape cooks used the contrasting flavour between salt and sweet; they served powdered salt with oranges, peaches, strawberries and melons; and every South African child who is well educated knows the improvement in the taste of a ripe quince when it is crushed on a rock with some sea-water and eaten with some of the brine adhering to the pulp.

We owe a debt of gratitude to our founder, Jan van Riebeeck, who was at pains from the day he landed to establish an orchard on the settlement, and who devoted much of his attention to introducing various fruits from the Fatherland. Within a few years it was possible to obtain many European fruits at the Cape and, later on, practically all visitors testified to the excellence of these. Lady Duff Gordon, who found little to praise in the Cape cuisine, waxed eloquent over the fruit-melons, figs, apples, peaches and apricots – that she bought so largely and so cheaply. Nelson, in his evidence before a Select Committee of the House of Commons, spoke of the beautiful grapes that grew so abundantly at the outpost that he did not think was of much strategic importance. Today matters are somewhat different. Our apples are no longer what they used to be, and we can import better ones from Canada; our peaches and apricots have increased in size and diminished in flavour; our oranges are . . . but let us be thankful that we still have many kinds of most excellent fruit, chief among which stand our grapes.

In preparing fruit for the table, the old Malay cooks drew on their experience with tropical fruit. They hardly ever boiled fruit in water; they recognised that most fruits contain enough water to allow gentle steaming if one wanted to cook them, while for preserves it was necessary to impregnate them with the thin syrup by slow and prolonged maceration under an equally gentle heat. Fresh fruit was served without any accompaniment, but there was always a cruet on the table with powdered salt, pepper, ginger and cinnamon, from which the guest, if he so desired, could help himself.

Fresh melon, for instance, was usually eaten with a little salt and pepper, though some diners preferred ginger, and others salt and cinnamon. Fruit was dried in the sun, on a rough scaffolding; sometimes it was peeled, sometimes the rind was left on; the seed or stone was always taken out, and large fruit were cut into slices. Very ripe fruit was sometimes pounded and spread in layers on paper or cloth and allowed to dry in the sun, a little salt being strewn on it. This makes the once very popular

fruits but now hardly ever seen *plat perskie* (flat peach) in which the dried layer of mashed ripe peach is rolled up or folded into a square for use when travelling. It has a sour-sweet, slightly saltish taste, is a great thirst quencher, and far more nourishing than any chewing gum.

Some fruits were dipped into lye before being dried; this was generally the case with grapes. No sulphur was used in the old days, and no one was particularly impressed by dried fruit that had a pale yellow colour such as today appears to be the chief consideration. The peeled dry peaches that came from the farms in the South Western Districts at the end of the past century were unsurpassed in flavour, but their kind is no longer obtainable.

No Malay cook made *jam* in the modern way, by boiling the fruit till its individual shape was merged into a stiff sweet puree; they insisted that even so sequacious and flaccid an ingredient like duneberries should retain as much of its original integrity as possible when boiled to make a jam. This, by the way, was always called a conserve.

Essentially their jam was fruit cooked gently in a thin syrup till the combination was so intimate that the syrup, as such, could no longer be distinguished and the whole had merged into a blend of fruit, fruit juice and sugar, varying in consistency but never so mushy that the fruit itself had disintegrated to an extent that destroyed its shape. They boiled it in a copper preserving pan that was kept scrupulously clean, and never scrupled to mix with it such flavourings as their experience had taught them would enhance the taste of the fruit that was its basic ingredient.

Great care was taken to skim the boiling liquid and to prevent burning, and considerable skill was necessary to detect when the risk of caramelisation was imminent (the stage of overboiling as it was called), just as expert knowledge was needed to surpass the underboiled stage when, if the process was regarded as completed and the jam bottled, it would inevitably crystallise.

A few jam recipes may be of interest.

Grape jam. Take any kind of grapes, not too ripe; pick the berries from the stalks, prick them with a needle, and place them for half an hour in salt water. Then put them in your pot, with a little cold water, just enough to cover them, and let them boil for a minute or two. Then add sugar, in amount half the weight of your grapes, a few featherings of cinnamon and a couple of inch-long pieces of ginger, and allow to simmer gently until the syrup has thickened round the grapes. Ladle out into jars, allow to get luke warm, and pour over melted butter or fat. It will keep for very long.

Quince jam. Peel your quinces and cut them into neat slices. Put them, with the cores, in a little salt water; dry and cook them in a little water and when they are soft, take out the cores. Now add your sugar, enough to equal the weight of the fruit, with your cinnamon, ginger and a blade of mace. Boil very slowly, skimming frequently and

taking care that it does not burn. If you wish you may add fruits
some moskonfyt to give it a colour (caramelised sugar does
just as well).

Later recipes, obviously under European influence, say
that the fruit should be "minced"; they also give directions
for making jams compounded of carrots, pumpkin,
squash and such like soft things, that make a sweet puree.
But the old cooks did not call these concoctions conserves, but spoke of them as a chutney or as a fruit puree,
or thick fruit sauce which was occasionally served warm
with meat dishes.

Chinese influence is equally obvious in the old methods
for preserving fruit whole or in pieces, in thin syrups.
This was also applied to some vegetables, just as in
China they preserved bamboo shoots. The fruit or vegetable, if it was soft, was after peeling put for a varying
length of time in brine or lime water, to harden its outside.
It was then gently parboiled and after that allowed to
simmer in the syrup, to which ginger, cinnamon, mace,
tangerine peel, or cloves were generally added. In a
few instances brandy or rum was added. The result aimed
at was to obtain a perfectly-translucent preserve, replete
with the original flavour of the fruit or vegetable but
blended with other flavourings that enhanced its pristine
virtue.

With fresh fruits, either whole or cut up, *fruit salads*
were made, always with a little sugar and wine. Indeed,
a fruit salad without wine was regarded as an exhibition
of bad taste. The flavourings used were nutmeg, cinnamon, rose water, lemon juice, almonds, tangerine peel,
preserved cumquats or citron, and occasionally rum or
brandy. Vanilla came into favour in the middle of the
nineteenth century, but the old cooks cordially detested
it and against the old-fashioned flavourings, it cuts a
very poor figure except in milk dishes where its peculiar,
thick floral perfume seems to be kept in proper check.
Even in these, however, nutmeg is less vulgar and more
satisfying.

Some notes on the various fruits, with such special
recipes as seem worthy of mention by reason of their
local modifications, may now be given.

fruits   *Apples*: These were baked, stewed, pureed, made into jam, open tarts, pies, salads and soups, according to the printed recipes. The only modification that seems to owe something to local influence (apart, of course, from the usual Cape methods of combining the fruit with spices and flavourings) is:

Baked apple. Choose large, not too ripe apples; wipe and core them; but you need not peel them as when baked your guests can easily remove the skins. Put the cores in water, with a stick of cinnamon, a blade of mace, some ginger and tangerine peel, and let them boil till the water becomes glutinous. Pour through a sieve and n ix with honey. Dust your apples, inside the core, with sugar and a little fine salt, and put them in a pan to bake in the oven; when they are soft, fill them with the honey mixture and let them bake for half an hour longer, basting them well with what drips from them. Serve up on fried bread.

Some recipes direct that the apples should be filled with guava jelly; one advises a mixture of almonds and pine kernels pounded in a mortar with tangerine peel and rose water. The apples are much better if they are peeled before being baked. All manner of variations may be played on this recipe.

Apricots were dried, preserved in salt as *meebos*, or in thin syrup; made into jam, salads, purees, pies, tarts and, more rarely, into soups. The kernels were always used as an addition to jam and sometimes as a flavouring for sweet dishes; the dried fruit was in great demand for chutneys, and the half-ripe apricots for *atjahrs*. The following is the recipe for making:

Meebos. Select your largest and very best apricots, which must be ripe enough to be soft but must still be firm. Do not peel them, but wipe them with a damp cloth to get rid of the bloom. Put them into thick brine and let them stay there for a day and a night. Then take them out; press out the stone from each one, and squeeze the pulp flat; strew some salt over and put them in the sun. Cover them with a damp cloth at night, but uncover them the next day to let the sun get at them. Do not make them too dry. When they are ready — which will be in four day's time — put them on a layer of sugar in a jar; sprinkle more sugar over, and put another layer of fruit; continue till the jar is filled, with a thick layer of sugar on top. It will keep like this for many months.

Meebos made like this is a delicious sour-salt-sweet-meat; the commercial variety, made from mixed pulp, is a very poor substitute. Miss Duckitt, who gives a later recipe for it, states that "it is a very nice sweetmeat and said to be a remedy for sea-sickness." She had her own way of preparing it, which was to crystallise the dried meebos in a thin syrup.

140

Cape gooseberries. These were sometimes served raw, **fruits** but more commonly used as an addition to fruit salads, fruit macedoines or fruit coupes. Cooked, they were made into jam, tarts, pies, purees and puddings, nearly always with the addition of cream and nutmeg. They were never dried, and seldom made into jelly for they contain very little fruit pectin.

Figs were dried, served fresh, made into salads, purees, jams, pies and tarts. Firm, well-grown but green figs were made into one of the finest preserves, which was prepared almost entirely in accordance with oriental methods.

Green fig preserve. Take the largest and firmest figs; scrape off the zest (thin outer covering) with a bit of glass and put the scraped fig immediately into salt water to which you may add a little lime water. Let them lie in it for two days; take out, wipe dry, and boil them very gently in a little cold water till they are soft. Take out and put them on a clean cloth, to drain. Make a thin syrup with sugar, water and a teaspoonful of rose water; put your figs in this when it is boiling and draw the pot aside and let them soak in it overnight. The next day boil them in it very slowly till they are quite translucent and have absorbed most, but not all, the juice. Bottle them at once and tie down with cloth dipped in brandy.

No spice or flavouring of any kind was used in this preserve, though later recipes make mention of mace, which is quite unnecessary. The fruit has a most delicious taste; it should be served with black coffee or a glass of sherry, both of which bring out its delicate, characteristic flavour. It should be firm, as translucent as a good fruit jelly, and as crisp as the best bits in a mixed Chinese chow-chow. When the syrup is allowed to crystallize round the fruit we get *crystallised green figs*, now also commercialised, but when home-made only slightly inferior to the preserve.

Cherries: These have always been scarce and – like the other smaller berry fruits, mulberries, loganberries, dune-berries, strawberries, and the much less well known rose apples or *djamboes* – were generally served fresh, in fruit salads, macedoines or coupes, with or without the addition of cream, wine, rum, spices and flavourings. Mulberries and raspberries were beaten up with cream, lemon juice and a few drops of rum, while strawberries were soaked in wine, dusted with nutmeg or a little fine salt but rarely served with cream. An excellent recipe is that for:

Mulberry pudding. Pick up those that have dropped off the tree and select others that are ready to fall; they are the ripest, for which you will need the least sugar. Remove their stalks and place the berries in a saucepan with half their weight of sugar, a piece of cinnamon, a bit of lemon, a piece of tangerine peel and a little red wine. Let it come to the boil; press through a sieve and replace in the sauce-

fruits pan. Cut up a stale white loaf into slices an inch thick; cut off the crust, and place the slices in a mould which you have coated with butter. Pour over it your mulberry syrup, and put on it a layer of the mulberry puree. Put on it more breadcrumbs and go on in this manner till you have filled the mould, putting on top a layer of bread, which you have drenched in the syrup.

Place on top a plate with a weight on it, and put the mould in a cool place overnight. Then take out the pudding and serve with a cold fruit sauce. You may also bake or steam it, but in that case it is better to butter the slices of crumb before you pour the puree over. Some people put bits of citron peel, pistachio nuts, almonds or preserved ginger between the layers, but these are not really necessary.

I agree. The pudding is excellent without any additional spicing, though a few drops of rum improves it.

Grapes and *currants*. These were used dried, by themselves or as additions to other dishes, fresh when in season, and cooked as jam, additions to salads and coupes, or as garnishes for fish and meat dishes. Hanepoot grapes were also preserved in brandy and sometimes in a thin syrup. Grape juice, partly fermented, was used as a yeast for bread and cake making; a similar yeast was made from raisins. Elf was sometimes dished up with a garnishing of grape berries, peeled and steamed in white wine. Unripe grapes, stewed with honey or sugar and spices, made a good filling for tarts and open pies. Currants were made into jam, but more commonly used in cakes and puddings.

Plums and *prunes* were dried or served as stewed fruit, or baked in pies and tarts, or made into jam. The favourite flavouring was ginger or tangerine peel.

Watermelon: This was always served fresh, being sliced longitudinally at the table, so that the slices fell away from the central section, known as the "crown", which was considered the best part. It was eaten by itself without flavouring and the flesh was never cooked. From the thick rind an excellent *watermelon konfyt* was made, by scraping off the green part with a bit of glass, steeping the rind in lime water, parboiling it, and then boiling it slowly in syrup, usually with some ginger, tangerine peel and a few cloves added. The result was an almost transparent green preserve, very crisp when well made, with a curious, nondescript flavour.

Melons, of which formerly the best was the large-sized, deeply ribbed *geel spanspek*, intensely fragrant, with pink flesh and extraordinarily sweet, were served fresh and eaten with salt, pepper or ginger. A preserve was made from the rind, usually much softer than that made from watermelon, dark brown in colour, and with no particular flavour. As an addition to fruit salads, melons were in great demand. The late variety, with a smooth white skin and green flesh, known as *winter spanspek*, was much smaller but deliciously flavoured, though by no means so fragrant.

Pawpaws: Common enough now, these were formerly

scarce, imported and regarded more as vegetables than **fruits** as fruits. Green pawpaws were made into soups and bredies. A little more ripe, they were stewed with honey or sugar, ginger and a bit of tangerine peel, making an excellent hot fruit dish. Nowadays pawpaw is usually served sliced and fresh with a lemon or a little sugar, according to the taste of the eater. The old cooks treated it like pumpkin, and all the recipes for pumpkin cookery can be tried with pawpaw.

Avocado pear is best eaten by itself with whatever condiment is desired. As a salad it is too clogging by itself, and should be mixed, sparsely, with other ingredients. It contains a great deal of pectin, which gives it a bland, almost soapy consistency, and it needs for its due appreciation the contrast of a strong sour or salt flavour. With sugar it agrees badly, and it never appears to harmonise with wine.

Lychees: These formerly came, dried, from China and were known as Tonkin raisins. They were expensive and were served at dessert at fashionable houses. I have eaten them with fillets of sole and, prepared by an old cook who claimed to be descended from a Chinese convict, as a stuffing for quails wrapped and grilled in fig leaves. Today they are easily obtainable as they are widely grown in Natal and the Transvaal, and we ought to make greater use of them in our cookery. They are admirable when stewed in white wine, with a blade of mace and a little tangerine peel, make a good tart, and are excellent in pies.

Oranges: The old "seedling orange" , the best of which came from the Clanwilliam district where they now have been supplanted by the far less juicy navel orange, was the most popular. It was indeed the only kind referred to in the recipes. They were used fresh in salads or by themselves, preserved whole or in quarters in syrup, or made into marmalade. A favourite way of serving them was:

143

fruits   *Baked oranges.* Slice off the top of the orange and loosen the pulp, removing some of the seeds. Dust with salt and bake in the oven. Serve with a little powdered cinnamon and sugar.

Orange juice was much used for making orange jelly and cold orange pudding, in which the stiffening substance was the pectin derived from sea-weed. As many fruit jellies were made with such sea-weed jelly as a basis, the recipe for it may be given.

Orange jelly. Soak two handfuls of dried seaweed in cold water till the weed has swelled out and is soft; boil it in two cupfuls of water with one cupful of wine; strain through a cloth. Whisk the white of four eggs to a stiff froth; beat their yolks with three ounces of sifted sugar, two cups of strained orange juice and a little grated orange rind, and incorporate in the sea-weed liquor; finally whip in the beaten egg white and pour into a wetted mould. Let it stand overnight and, when turned out, serve with a garnish of orange segments and slices of preserved citron.

The sea-weed liquor is practically a strong solution o f pectin, which sets to a firm jelly when it gets cold. It has a curious taste – which is neither astringent nor woody, but between the two – and must be improved by some stronger and better-flavoured agent. It is merely a stiffening substance, but is cheap, easily made and acts as well as gelatine or isinglass. Although the latter was much used for jellies (as it was one of the chief means of fining wine) sea-weed was preferred by many old cooks as it was said to solidify better and to be exempt from the enzyme action of some fruits like pine-apple that interferes with the setting of animal gelatine.

Lemons, cumquats, pomelos and *tangerines*: All these are common, but, apart from their use as flavouring and sometimes as ingredients in salads, they are served only as fresh fruit, with the exception of the first two that are too tart to be eaten at table. Both cumquats and tangerines make an excellent preserve when boiled in syrup; neither needs any additional flavouring. Tangerine peel, dried, is extensively used as a flavouring for puddings, stewed fruits and suchlike things. It imparts a subtle, aromatic taste that combines excellently with anything that is sweet. The rind of the pomelo, or shaddock, like that of the large citron, makes a beautiful preserve with a flavour that is altogether its own. None of these citrus fruits is particularly useful for tarts or pies, although all are sometimes used for that purpose in combination with other fruits.

Guavas are such highly-fragrant and strong-tasting fruit that it is always better to use them in combination, although stewed guavas, made with a little cinnamon and ginger, and served with a sweet custard or plenty of cream, need not be despised. They are excellent in a:

Guava salad. Peel and slice large, fully-ripe guavas;

144

those with pink flesh are to be preferred and you must remove as many of the pips as you can. Mix them with peeled
and sliced oranges, a few tangerine wedges and peeled
and sliced bananas; strew over powdered sugar and let
them stand for a while in a cool place. Pour over a wineglass of sherry or white wine, give the salad a stir, dust with
grated nutmeg and serve.

As with all other fruit salads, there are many variations
of this recipe; some folk add shelled nuts, diced pawpaws,
peeled grapes, or even chopped citron and other preserved peels. One of the best additions is rose apple,
broken and bruised. The salad is sufficient in itself, but
is generally served with a cold custard or with whipped
cream.

Loquats: These are eaten fresh or stewed, with or
without spices. Tangerine peel goes well with them and
so does ginger. They make a good jam and a fairly well-
flavoured preserve.

Pomegranates were formerly much more in favour
than they are today. They were used to stuff meat, in the
Oriental manner, and as garnishes. The modern cook has
not much use for them and their preparation entails an
amount of labour that can be devoted to better purpose.

Limes or *lemmetjies* make a glorious pickle and their
juice, when mixed with rum, some nutmeg and sugar
and broken ice, provides one of the finest drinks that one
can wish for on a hot day. They are also preserved in
syrup or salt.

Olives, although grown at the Cape, have never been
extensively used. The old recipes are silent about them,
although they are mentioned in one that gives directions
for stuffing pigeons with a farce in which chopped olives
is an ingredient. The wild olive has a tiny, acrid, and almost
useless fruit.

Peaches: The ripe fruit is served by itself or stewed with
a little white wine and sugar. The dried is perhaps the
favourite for a stewed fruit dish, and the following recipe
may serve as a generic one:

Stewed dried peaches. Soak them in water and when
they have swelled, take them out and dry them on a damp
cloth; put them in a saucepan with half a cupful of sugar, a
few featherings of cinnamon, a bit of dried tangerine peel,
and a little grated lemon peel. Pour over a cup of sweet red
wine, and put the saucepan where it can simmer gently.
Shake it from time to time, but do not stir. When ready,
serve up hot or cold as you prefer.

To make it perfect one should add a few crushed peach
and apricot kernels.

Nectarines are dealt with exactly in the same way as
peaches. Both are sometimes served as fritters. They are
peeled, halved, the stone taken out and each half dusted
with sugar, ginger and cinnamon; they are then dipped
in a sweet batter and fried in boiling fat. Orange slices,
pineapple and other fruits that lend themselves to similar

145

fruits treatment, may be fried in the same way.

Quinces are treated like apples. They make an excellent sambal, jelly and bredie.

Custard apple is always eaten by itself, but as an addition to a fruit salad it is excellent.

Bananas and *plantains:* These were known from the earliest times and there has always been a keen demand for them. They were served by themselves, baked, fried, stewed, made into puddings, jellies, salads or purees, but were never served plainly boiled as they sometimes are in the East. In their cooked form they are perhaps best when fried in fat, and fried bananas were regarded as indispensable when serving soesaties or a hot curry.

Mangoes were used only for chutneys and were rarely available on the market, which probably accounts for their relatively infrequent mentions in the old recipes.

Jack fruit, which is now cultivated in Natal and the Transvaal, can scarcely be considered a fruit. It is a most delicate vegetable for its flesh, when steamed with a little butter, approaches in flavour and delicacy that of well-grown asparagus or *couer de palmier.* Its large black seeds can be roasted like chestnuts, to which they approximate in taste.

The fruit of the *prickly pear,* when fully ripe and properly denuded of thorns, is sapid, aromatic and pleasant to the taste, but is rarely used in cookery.

That of the *Hottentot fig,* about which botanists are not yet agreed as to whether it properly can be called a fruit, is eaten by children. Lady Duff Gordon found it too sour for her taste. It makes, however, a good jam.

Rose apples, or *djamboes,* are very aromatic, and their usefulness as flavouring agents is not yet appreciated; they are best as a preserve.

Grenadillas are best served beaten up with sugar, cream and wine, or as a water or cream ice.

There are many kinds of indigenous fruits, mainly berries, that are edible. So far they have not been popularised in cookery, although some of them have great possibilities.

There are no recipes among my old manuscripts for making water or cream ices. The reason for this is obvious, namely the want of ice or of refrigerating machinery in these far off days. Ice cream was well known at the time when the Cape was first occupied, but it was prepared with the aid of stored ice which was not available at the Cape. It is equally obvious that the juices of all our Cape fruits can be used for making water and cream ices, as well as for making fruit drinks, for which recipes will be found in all printed cookery books.

As far as I have been able to ascertain, all our recipes for fruit drinks are copies of old European directives, with a few unimportant modifications, chiefly in the use of spices and additional flavourings. The "harvest drink" mentioned by Miss Duckitt is a case in point; it is nothing but a variety of the age-old mulled wine that is described in the old cook books.

146

Chapter XIV

ODDS AND ENDS

THE old recipes deal slightingly with milk. Its food value was to some extent dependent on its preparation and our forefathers, perhaps very properly, felt that if it was made into cheese it was of greater value to the community than when it was drunk as a liquid. Here are some of the ways in which they recommended that it should be prepared for the table.

Bread-and-milk. Take a piece of stale white bread and cut it into dice; pour over it a pint of boiling milk in which you have melted a teaspoonful of butter, and dissolved a tablespoonful of sugar or honey. Grate nutmeg over and serve.

Milk brawn. Into a cupful of sea-weed liquid stir two cupfuls of hot milk, which you have boiled up with a feathering of cinnamon, a cupful of sugar and a blade of mace. Pour into a wetted mould, and when set turn out and serve with cream.

Sago milk. Boil a cupful of sago in three cupfuls of milk with half a cupful of sugar or honey and a feathering of cinnamon or a piece of dried tangerine peel. Pour into a dish, grate nutmeg over, and serve. You may also bake it in the oven.

Fat milk. Boil three cupfuls of new milk with an ounce of suet, half a cupful of honey or sugar, and a little grated fresh lemon peel. Pour through a sieve and serve with a dusting of grated nutmeg.

Toast and milk. Toast a slice of stale white bread; butter it and pour over it boiled milk that you have thickened with a little rice flour and to which you have added a lump of butter and a pinch of salt. Serve very hot.

Milk also enters into some of the old-fashioned drinks that were served on cold winter nights.

Milk and wine. Boil a cup of wine with half a cup of milk; when it boils stir in two wineglassfuls of white wine; let it boil up; remove and set aside to cool; then pour off the whey that floats on top; mix with sugar and spices according to your taste. Serve hot or cold, as best pleases you.

Another foodstuff that was a favourite with the old cooks was flour in some form or other. Wheat flour was extensively used; barley, oats and rye and other cereals, including mielies, were at first not too popular. It was only in the nineteenth century that mielie meal became the staple food of the poorer class. It was prepared in much the same way as that in which the first settlers had made their flour "paps" or porridges of various cereals. Such paps are usually served with milk and sugar; sometimes a piece of butter is added to each plate. Oatmeal was rarely used, and then always with a good deal of salt added; it was sometimes baked in the oven and then made into a porridge and served with cream and honey. Kaffircorn porridge was a much later development. Mielie flour was never granulated, and it is worth noting that we have no local recipe for polenta or semolina.

Raisin mielies (gestampte mielies). Take dried mielies and wet them slightly. Put them in a wooden mortar and pound them lightly, so that they break and their husk comes off. Put them in water to remove the husks which will float, and let them soak. Take them out when they have swelled a little and put them in a saucepan, with some salt, half a cupful of sugar, two cupfuls of stalked and seeded raisins and a few featherings of cinnamon; add some water and let the mielies simmer slowly, stirring often. When they are soft and pasty, turn out and serve.

Although the mielies are broken, the fragments should retain their individuality in this dish and should be mixed intimately with the raisins, cohering to them by virtue of the gruellike consistency that the mielies should have when properly cooked. This dish, which is not regarded as a dessert dish but served with meats, may be made much richer and more like a pudding, by adding cream, spices and a few drops of rum to it. From a nutrition point of view it is far more nourishing than any other mielie dish.

Bread was made with or without yeast. All visitors to the Cape who wrote before the nineteenth century and make mention of it, declare that the brown and white bread that they tasted here was excellent. The wheat

flour was crushed between stones; brown bread was **odds**
baked with the whole-wheat flour; for the white bread, **& ends**
the flour was sifted. The brown bread as made by Malay
cooks was delightful when it was fresh and moist; when
a few days old it was not so good. Their white bread
was of various degrees of refinement, but never ap-
proached the thin, wooden consistency of white, steam-
baked bread. It was nearly always slightly granular and,
from a dietetic point of view, was quite as nourishing as
their brown bread.

Bread was baked, usually, in an outside brick oven;
only later was it prepared in an iron kitchen oven. A
magnificent variety was baked in a pot, with hot coals
on the lid and this was regarded, quite rightly, as the
test of the artist's skill in baking bread. For yeast they
used partly-fermented must, crushed raisins, fermented
dough, or dried hops and sometimes an indigenous plant
that has similar properties.

Potato yeast (*aartappelsuurdeeg*). Take a teacupful of
dried hops and boil it in a quart of water with a pound of
peeled and diced potatoes; let it cool and add to it half a
cupful of flour, three tablespoonsful of sugar mixed in a
pint of water. Cover it closely and let it stand for a day and
a night, when it will be ready for use.

Raisin yeast. Pound up two cups of raisins and put
them in a wide-mouthed jar which you fill with water in
which you have dissolved a little sugar. In a couple of
days, when the raisins rise to the top, it will be fit for use.

Meal yeast (*soet suurdeeg*). Take a yeast pot (any
earthenware jar with a closely-fitting lid) and fill it half
full with boiling water; put in, without stirring, two cups of
unsifted wheat flour and a teaspoonful of sugar and cover
it so that none of the moisture can escape. Let it stand in a
warm place on the hearth overnight and add to it a cupful
of hot water the next day, give it a stir, and let it remain till
it begins to bubble and work, when you can use it.

Some recipes add salt to the brew, but there seems to
be no reason for this and the flour will ferment quite well
— indeed better — without it.

Old yeast (*ou suurdeeg*) is simply a portion of the
dough put aside in the yeast pot, which always contains
spores of the yeast mould, mixed with lukewarm water
and allowed to ferment. It is a convenient way of making
yeast, but is stated to give a heavier loaf than the other
yeast varieties.

The mixture of flour and water or some other liquid produced various kinds of dough and batter, and the directions for preparing these different kinds are usually precise. As a matter of fact, they differ in no way from those
that were already in print in the early part of the seventeenth century and they lay emphasis on precisely the
same points that the best European cooks had insisted
on in making dough — the necessity to keep it cool, to

handle it as little as possible and to allow it to settle.
A plain water dough was used for pies and simple tarts ; an egg dough, much more complicated and resembling the French *feuilletage*, was invariably used for sweet tarts. The best cooks rolled it out 24 times, adding a little fresh butter each time, with the result that the subsequent baked layers were as thin as tissue paper and when, properly baked, as crisp yet as deliciously melting as a slither of crackling.

For the spongy dough, that required a good yeast, the recipe was almost exactly that given in the old printed books for what is now known as baba mixture. It produced a soft, pudding-like result, that was invariably served with moskonfyt instead of the ordinary rhum syrup.

Another variety was transparent dough, made exclusively with butter and thrice-sifted flour, and so repeatedly rolled that my unmathematical mind boggles at the task of computing the number of final layers. Baking powder and bicarbonate of soda were never used ; they are first mentioned in recipes dating from the latter part of the eighteenth century and, although it must frankly be admitted that they have lightened the task of the cook, the doughs made without them suffered no less from their omission.

There were several "secret" processes connected with the preparation of doughs and generally with cake making that certain conservative cooks jealously guarded. These were never committed to paper but were preserved by oral tradition. Some of them were not worth all the fuss that was made about them, a few were of such a nature that no self-respecting cook would ever have employed them (as, for instance, one method of getting a fine patina on darioles and tartlets) while others were really of value. The manner of making "filled pancakes", secret of my old preceptress with the wooden spoon, for example, was apparently unknown to other Cape Town cooks.

Filled pancakes (gevulde pannekoek). Make a pancake batter with thrice-sifted flour, a very little rice flour, the yolk, well-whipped, of two large eggs, and enough white wine to produce a thin batter that flows easily off your spoon. Whip it well and place it aside for a couple of hours before it is wanted. For your filling you want a couple of blanched sweet and one bitter almond, two pistachio nuts and a tablespoonful of peeled pine kernels. Pound these in a mortar with a tablespoonful of butter, a few drops of rose water and a little powdered tangerine peel, and add to it a teaspoonful of honey, working the mixture till it is a stiff cream. Thin it slightly by adding more butter till it is of a consistency to spread easily. Put some butter or fat in your pan, add a little salt to your batter and pour into the pan enough of it to make a very thin pancake. As soon as it is browned on the underside, coat it quickly with your filling mixture, fold it and put it on a hot dish ; go on till you have enough pancakes. Pour them over a glass of rum and good brandy mixed, set it alight and serve at once.

Speaking from an experience that extends over 40 years, I can honestly say that I have never eaten more delicious pancakes than these, and that the European crepe suzette, of later invention, is a bad second to them. My old Malay woman made them so crisp and knife-edge thin that it seems impossible to fold them, yet she managed to do it with a dexterity that I envied and have never been able to imitate successfully.

There were, of course, many other recipes for pancakes with something or other inside them, and serving them with flaming rum and brandy was a common practice. The usual pancake batter was made with flour, egg yolk and milk, with a little sugar and salt added, and was served with powdered cinnamon, nutmeg and sugar mixed. It was never tossed, but always deftly turned, although it was usually made so thin that both sides were cooked without the necessity to turn it. The cinnamon and sugar was dusted on its upper surface, it was rolled up and sent to table with a halved lemon for each guest — never a slice or a quarter.

Thicker pancakes were favoured by some cooks; in these the batter was mixed with various ingredients such as herbs and spices.

A salt omelet-like pancake was sometimes served with roast meat, for Yorkshire pudding was a much later introduction.

An old favourite, that has retained its popularity though it is now usually steam-baked and is even made from the horrible flour that cooks are not allowed to sift, is:

Raisin bread (*rosyntjie brood*). Make a dough with flour, salt, sugar, powdered cinnamon, grated nutmeg and a few cumin seeds. Add some raisin yeast and put aside in a cool place covered with a wet cloth; when it rises add stoned raisins and a cupful of good fat; knead well, shape into loaves and bake in the oven.

This, rather vague, original recipe does not give the amounts; few of the Malay cooks stipulated how much of each ingredient should be used and the reader was left in doubt on this point. It was presumed, apparently, that the intending maker of the dish knew for how many guests it would have to serve and could apportion the quantities as desired. Nowadays baking powder is used instead of yeast, and raisin bread becomes almost a Boston bread sort of cake, heavy and moist. In its original form it was, and should always be, delightfully crusty outside, and beautifully crumbly within. When fresh from the oven and still hot it is delicious eaten with butter.

Ash cakes (*as koek*) which is really a kind of unleavened damper was made as follows.

How to make good as-koek. It is better to sift your meal, for that makes the cake whiter, but if you cannot do so you may use unsifted meal. Mix it with enough salt to give it a good taste and stir it into milk or buttermilk till it is firm enough to knead. Add to it some tail fat and knead it well.

151

It is not necessary to use yeast, but if you want it to rise like bread you may put some fermented must in with it, if you happen to make it in the time of wine-harvesting. Let it stand awhile before you use it. You must form it into cakes the size of your palm and about half an inch thick, and bake it on the gridiron. It is good eaten with fat or butter.

It is good eaten with anything, in fact, though perhaps best with butter and cheese, but it must be served very hot. It is the usual damper prepared in camp, where the flour is now commonly mixed with soda or baking powder. A coarse variety, known as *stormjaers* or *attackers*, is made by simply mixing meal with water and a little soda and baking the cakes in hot embers. It is filling, but leaves much to be desired from a culinary point of view.

Citron bread was made in much the same way as raisin bread, but is hardly known today. Preserved citron peel was cut into dice and was incorporated in a bread dough yeasted with fermenting must; usually ginger, tangerine peel and currants were added, and the result was really a not-too-sweet fruit cake. Gingerbread, which was another old favourite, was made in accordance with the old European recipes; the only modification seems to have been the use of tangerine peel.

Citron omelet. Chop up an ounce of preserved citron peel with a handful of stoned raisins and a little tangerine peel; mix it well with three beaten eggs; add a small glass of sweet white wine. Pour into a flat pan in which you have melted a little fat or butter, and let it set well; fold in two; scatter fine sugar over and serve.

Fried bread (*wentel teefies*). Cut slices of bread from a white loaf that is a week old or more, about a quarter of an inch thick and do not take away the crust. Soak them in buttermilk or, if you have no buttermilk, then in ordinary cold milk to which you have added a little white wine. Take out and drain. Then put each slice in some egg that you have beaten up well with a little salt; take out the bread and fry it on both sides in hot fat; strew cinnamon and sugar on each slice and serve.

Tarts were a feature in old Cape cookery. They were really open pies and were imitations of the old-fashioned Dutch *taart* (which itself was an imitation of the earlier, uncovered pies that probably came from the East) like the modern American "pies". Though there are many recipes for their preservation, some (indeed in the oldest printed cookery book extant) show interesting modifications.

Potato tart. Take mashed potatoes, two good cupfuls, a cupful of sugar or half a cupful of honey, half a dozen fresh eggs, half a pound of blanched almonds, a few bitter almonds and a couple of peach kernels, peeled; a pinch of powdered tangerine peel and a little salt. Pound the nuts with the sugar, peel and salt. Whip the yolks and whites of the eggs separately, with a little rosewater added to each. Mix the potatoes with the beaten yolk and pounded nuts and whip in the beaten whites. Line a dish with tart or pie dough, pour in the mixture and bake in the oven.

This mixture was sometimes put into a cloth and boiled as a pudding, or into a greased tin and baked in the oven.

Tarts were usually made with a very rich dough, repeatedly rolled and buttered, so that when baked it was exceedingly crisp and mellow. With this a deep soup plate was lined and the filling of the tart, which was its principal ingredient, was poured in. A decorated band of dough was placed on top as an edging and strips of dough were laid across the top in lattice fashion; these were brushed with yolk of egg and a little brandy before being baked to give the pastry a good golden colour; some cooks added a little saffron to the egg yolk.

The main thing in all tarts was the filling and for this there were many recipes. Probably the simplest was a fruit puree or jam, without any admixture. The best was undoubtedly the old-fashioned milk or custard filling, modified from the old Italian recipes in so many different ways that almost every cook had his, or her, own way of making it – and thoroughly despised anybody else's method. They were all very tasty, being good-baked custards intensively flavoured and sinfully rich.

A milk tart. Boil two pints of milk with a feathering of cinnamon, a bit of dried tangerine peel, a teaspoonful of honey and half a cupful of coconut milk, one bitter almond, shelled and blanched, and one peach kernel. Beat three egg yolks with a little candy sugar and stir them into the boiling milk; take off and pour through a sieve; add another egg beaten up with the whites of the three eggs and a small glass of sweet wine, and whisk well. Pour into the lined tart dish and bake fairly quickly in the oven.

Another milk tart. Take coconut milk, new milk and cream, of each an equal portion, and whip them well with a pinch of salt, the yolks of four eggs, a little grated nutmeg and a little powdered tangerine peel. When they are well beaten, add honey or sugar to sweeten; put the mixture on the fire and stir till it thickens, but do not let it boil. Then pour into your mould and bake. Sprinkle cinnamon and nutmeg on top.

A rich milk tart. You may make this by pounding in a mortar a handful of blanched sweet and one bitter almond with a few apricot or peach kernels, three tablespoonsful of sugar candy, a teaspoonful of rice flour, some flicks of mace and a bit of dried tangerine peel, which mixture you must wash with coconut milk through a sieve. With what comes through you must mix its own amount of cream skimmed from the morning's milk, and the yolk of as many eggs as will equal it in weight. When you have well mixed these you may add, also, the white and yolk of one egg beaten up with a glass of brandy or sweet wine. This you pour into the pie dish, which you have lined with paste rolled out 14 times at least, and you must bake it quickly in a hot oven. When done you may put on top of it some grated nutmeg and little crosses made of citron peel.

Coconut tart was made in the same way, its main ingredient being grated fresh coconut. *Nut tart* had a rich, juicy filling of pounded almonds, pistachios, pine kernels and walnuts, mingled with cream and egg yolk.

Pumpkin, squash and *vegetable marrow tart* were simply made with fillings of pureed vegetables. There was a special kind of such a gourd tart that needed a preliminary cooking, which was generally so good that it was served without waiting to put it in a tart.

Baked vegetable marrow. Pare and dice the marrow, which must not be too ripe. Put it in a pie dish with butter, sugar, cinnamon, nutmeg and a little tangerine peel. Bake it in the oven till it turns brown.

Although this was properly a filling for pies, it was used as a dish by itself; a little watery though it be, it tastes very well, and its liquidity may be much lessened by incorporating bits of toasted bread or dried breadcrumbs in it before it is baked. It is one of the easiest and nicest ways to prepare any of the gourd tribe of vegetables.

Closed pies were not usually sweet dishes, the word *pastei* being reserved, by usage though not by idiom, to pasties filled with some vegetable or animal material without sugar or honey. Piecrust dough differed in no way from rich tart dough; for the more moist kind of pies, a batter, that yielded a dumpling-like result, was sometimes used. The dumpling doughs were varied, and some recipes were, like those for milk tart, considered to be family heirlooms. Again, as a matter of fact, they differ in no way from old printed recipes.

Dumplings or *kluitjies,* considered as sweet dishes and

not as meat, fish or vegetable farce boiled in soup or **odds** hashes, were made from a dough that was shaped into **& ends** balls, pressed through a colander (in that way resembling the old-fashioned Hungarian *taronyha*) or rolled out and cut into strips, like Chinese noodles. They were then boiled, usually in milk, and served with sugar and cinnamon, or with a sweet sauce. The simplest dough was one made with water, egg yolk, butter, sugar and a little spice; a more elaborate one was where the dough was finally mixed with the whisked egg white, this yielding a more friable, sponge-like dumpling. Where no sugar was added to the dough, it could be used for dumplings suitable to accompany meat, soup, or vegetables. Typical recipes are:

Milk dumplings (*melk kluitjies or melk frummeltjies*). Into a pint and a half of boiling milk stir two tablespoonfuls of butter, a little salt and two cupfuls of well-sifted flour, till you have a gruel-like paste; let it cool and beat into it three eggs; shape this dough into small balls and cook in boiling milk till they float. Take out, dust with sugar and cinnamon or nutmeg, and serve.

Into this dough may be incorporated currants, raisins, dates, or anything else you like; the dumplings also can be added to any meat dish. The dough may be rolled out and cut into thin strips, or pressed through a colander, and these strips and droppings boiled in milk, soup, or wine and served as a dish by themselves – with a sweet sauce for dessert, or with a vegetable puree or gravy sauce, as a savoury dish.

Rice dumplings. Mash wet boiled rice to a paste with eggs, rich flour and butter and a pinch of salt. Cook in boiling water, take out, drain and serve with a dusting of sugar and spice, or with a gravy sauce. Here, too, you may incorporate into the dumpling whatever dried or preserved fruit you fancy if you want a sweet dish, or add a herb flavouring if you wish to serve the dumplings with a meat dish or a soup.

A richer variety of dumpling was made with rice flour, cream, butter, egg yolk, honey and spices; a coarser one simply with flour, milk and salt. The main point was that the product should be light, porous and neither granular nor flaky but something between both. As a dish for a cold winter's evening, dumplings boiled in milk and served with sugar and cinnamon were regarded as a generally acceptable finish to the dinner or supper. At the Cape they supplied, to a great extent, the need for farinaceous additions to a meal that in Italian cookery is met by the many varieties of *pasta*.

An interesting variation of such cookery is that in which Oriental influence is plainly apparent. Malay cooks, in their native country, were in the habit of making nut and farinaceous, and sometimes fruit doughs, boiling or frying them in fat, and preserving them, sometimes for

months, in honey or thick syrup made by evaporating
fruit juices. Such delicacies, coloured with ochre, turmeric
or saffron, heavily-spiced and inordinately sweet, may
still be bought in Indian bazaars. Occidental taste usually
considers them too cloyingly nectarious specially when
they are heavily perfumed.

In South Africa one kind, which is a trifle more in har-
mony with western ideas, has survived in:

Koeksisters. To three cups of sifted flour add one cup of
moist brown sugar, a teaspoonful of ground cinnamon, half
a teaspoonful of ground ginger, of cloves, of allspice and of
tangerine peel, a little salt, four well-beaten eggs and
enough melted fat to make it into a thick dough. Add some
raisin yeast and knead it well in; cover with a wet cloth
and let it stand until it has risen. Cut small finger-thin strips
from it, roll them into figures of eight and boil them in
boiling fat. Take out when they are puffed and brown and
drain.

Then put them, while they are still hot, into thick syrup,
flavoured with almonds, cinnamon or whatever you like.
Take out after an hour and drain. They can be served as
soon as they are cool, but can be kept for weeks and are
better when they are a few days old.

The most delicious koeksisters are those made with rice
flour and saturated in a syrup made by boiling nutmeg,
while it still has its original covering of mace, with sugar.
They are golden coloured, translucent, and highly-
aromatic. They should be well drained in any case and
should never be greasy.Today they are most commonly
immersed in a syrup in which green figs, citron or tangerines have been preserved, and are never perfumed or
coloured.

Eastern influence is also apparent in the recipe for:

Sweet cakes (*soet koekies*). Make a dough with four
pounds of flour mixed with two pounds of moist brown
sugar, a pound of creamed butter, half a pound of soft
tail-fat, a little salt and a wineglassful of brandy. Pound
four handfuls of blanched almonds, a few bitter almonds
and a few peach kernels, in a mortar with a quarter of an
ounce of powdered cloves and the same quantity of
powdered cinnamon; mix them with four eggs and a little
red ochre powder, with some raisin yeast, and knead them
into the dough. Let it stand for 24 hours. Then roll out thin
and cut into shapes with a cup or knife; butter a large
pan and set your cakes in it; put a piece of preserved ginger
or citron on top of each cake; bake them in a quick oven
for half an hour.

They were served with wine or coffee, and were very
popular. Nowadays they are made without the almonds
and with soda and are a poor imitation of the originals,
which were a fine cross between a macaroon and an
Oriental fruit cake. In one recipe the nut content is increased by the addition of pine kernels, which seems to

156

be an improvement as it makes them more flaky; another modification is to add honey.

There were various sweetmeats, most of them emanating from the East. One of the earliest things I was taught to make was the age old *tameletjie*, a kind of rock much in favour with all Cape children in the days when sweets were all home-made. It was prepared as follows:

Tameletjies. Take a cup of brown sugar, a lump of butter the size of a hen's egg, half a cupful of water and a pinch of salt; make a syrup that will "crackle" when dropped into cold water. Have ready blanched, split almonds, some grated tangerine peel and a little cinnamon; fold pieces of paper into little square pannikins, smear them inside with fat, and put some almonds, cinnamon and peel inside each; pour the syrup on them and, when it is half set, put more almonds, peel and cinnamon in. When hard take off the paper.

We used various kinds of nuts, chiefly pine kernels but sometimes the soft, fragrant embryos of leucodendron seeds, for this sweet, and simply mixed all the ingredients in the syrup, which was then poured on to a buttered tin — the lid of a biscuit tin served admirably — and cut into pieces when set. It is really a highly-spiced toffee, or better, a rock sweet, but more variegated than the ordinary almond rock. Some old Malay cooks made an interesting variation of it, in which "butter nuts", the seeds of an indigenous melon, scraps of dates and a little moskonfyt were mingled with the almonds.

Another favoured sweetmeat was made with almond paste, rose water, citron preserve finely minced, powdered cinnamon and allspice and tangerine peel, sugar and honey, all beaten up with egg white. It could be baked as a sort of macaroon by itself, or enclosed in a coating of tart dough and either fried in fat or baked in the oven. Malay cooks were fond of flavouring these cakes with some perfume and, later on, vanilla was largely used for this purpose.

There seems to be no recipes for preserving flowers, although such delicacies were well known in Europe and in the East. My old Malay cook crystallised wild jasmine flowers — then common enough, but now rare — by slightly steaming them and then immersing them in a crystallising syrup made of sugar, green ginger and a pinch of salt. They looked rather draggled, but retained something of their fragrance and tasted, to children at least, very nice. Orange and lemon flowers were dealt with in the same way; gourd flowers were sometimes fried in fat and served with a dusting of powdered sugar and cinnamon.

Similarly the old manuscript recipes for *cheese dishes* seem to be mere copies of European originals. Cheese was made on some farms, but it was usually eaten fresh, with bread and butter, and was not even of much account as an addition to farinaceous and vegetable dishes. There are a few recipes for cheese puddings and cheese *vlae* or custard. Miss Duckitt gives several of these, but though they make savoury dishes they differ in no way from those already in print at the time. A little-known, but by no means locally original, way of treating cheese is the following:

Chilli cheese. Pound three ounces of cheese in a mortar with a tablespoonful of powdered chillies, a tablespoonful of butter, a teaspoonful of powdered ginger and a pinch of salt. Whisk into it enough cream to make into a thin paste, to which add a well-beaten egg; put the mixture in a buttered pie dish and steam or bake it. Serve with a sweet chutney.

This is a fiery, cheerfully-biting, custardy dish, to which some cooks add a bit of saffron to give it a lemon colour. Its pungency is perhaps too forcible for most people's taste, but a sweet chutney, or a semi-sweet dish like stewed sweet potatoes, does a great deal to enhance its merits.

To use up old ship's cheese. Collect all the stray scraps you can find; do not reject those that are mouldy. Pound them well in a mortar with powdered pepper, mace, ginger and cloves; add enough brandy in which you have steeped verbena and sweet thyme leaves to make it into a thick paste; if you have a little sour cream, add it too; let it stand for a few days, when it will become mouldy; mix it well once more, adding more brandy, and fill a wide-mouthed jar with it. You may use it on bread or biscuits, for it will keep for a long time.

This is a very tasty and aromatic spiced cheese, which is improved by the addition of a little moist sugar, but certainly spoiled by adding mustard. It is, however, merely a variant of dozens of recipes for potted cheese, and has no claim to be South African, although it comes from an old Cape manuscript cook book.

Nothing has been said about drinks, for the simple reason that those mentioned in the seventeenth and eighteenth century recipes at the Cape are all familiar to European cooks. This may be surprising to many who maintain, for instance, that there are special South African ways of making coffee. That is a fallacy. "Coffee was hardly known at the Cape in the seventeenth century; it certainly never came here with Van Riebeeck", as one writer observes, and it is improbable that our Founder ever served it at the Castle to his family or his guests. Its use was restricted in Holland till 1680 and only after that date do we find mention of it at the Cape. *Coffee imports from Java were of much later date. Our methods of making coffee have nothing that is essentially different

*Coffee plants were introduced in Java and were also sent to the Cape at the end of the seventeenth century. Coffee was actually produced on some Cape farms in the eighteenth and nineteenth centuries but, like indigo, its cultivation was not an economic success.

from those used in the early part of the eighteenth century in European coffee houses.

There, too, they roasted the beans with a little fat, pounded them immediately before making coffee (grinding machines came in much later) and added salt, or a pinch of sweet herbs (later, by some foul mischance, changed to mustard) to the brew, which was always made with boiling water and, to settle the ground, sometimes used a hot poker or a burning brand, exacly as we still do in our camp cookery.

They also served sweet cakes and conserves with coffee, as that was merely a continuation of the custom of serving them with a glass of wine drunk in the forenoon or afternoon. There is thus nothing of particular interest in our coffee making methods, and so far as I have been able to discover, we have no other drinks that have any justification to claim a local origin.

METRICATION: The author did not choose to give specific and detailed lists of ingredients for the recipes in this book. To retain the flavour of the original text it has not been metricated and such terms as 'pound' or 'ounce' are occasionally found.
(One pound = 453 grams; one ounce = 28 grams)